D0000987

THE COMPLETE GUIDE TO WIKIS:

How to Set Up, Use, and Benefit From Wikis for Teachers, Business Professionals, Families, and Friends

By T. Brian Chatfield

The Complete Guide to Wikis: How to Set Up, Use, and Benefit From Wikis for Teachers, Business Professionals, Families, and Friends

Copyright © 2009 Atlantic Publishing Group, Inc.
1405 SW 6th Avenue • Ocala, Florida 34471 • Phone 800-814-1132 • Fax 352-622-1875
Web site: www.atlantic-pub.com • E-mail: sales@atlantic-pub.com
SAN Number: 268-1250

ISBN-13: 978-1-60138-319-8   ISBN-10: 1-60138-319-3

Library of Congress Cataloging-in-Publication Data

Chatfield, T. Brian, 1984-
 The complete guide to wikis : how to set up, use, and benefit from wikis for teachers, business
professionals, families, and friends / by T. Brian Chatfield.
     p. cm.
Includes bibliographical references and index.
ISBN-13: 978-1-60138-319-8 (alk. paper)
ISBN-10: 1-60138-319-3 (alk. paper)
1. Wikis (Computer science) I. Title.
 TK5105.8882.C53 2009
 006.7'5--dc22
                              2009025919

Printed in the United States

PROJECT MANAGER: Erin Everhart • eeverhart@atlantic-pub.com
INTERIOR DESIGN: James Ryan Hamilton • james@jamesryanhamilton.com
JACKET DESIGN: Holly Marie Gibbs • hgibbs@atlantic-pub.com

We recently lost our beloved pet "Bear," who was not only our best and dearest friend but also the "Vice President of Sunshine" here at Atlantic Publishing. He did not receive a salary but worked tirelessly 24 hours a day to please his parents. Bear was a rescue dog that turned around and showered myself, my wife Sherri, his grandparents Jean, Bob, and Nancy and every person and animal he met (maybe not rabbits) with friendship and love. He made a lot of people smile every day.

We wanted you to know that a portion of the profits of this book will be donated to The Humane Society of the United States. – *Douglas & Sherri Brown*

The human-animal bond is as old as human history. We cherish our animal companions for their unconditional affection and acceptance. We feel a thrill when we glimpse wild creatures in their natural habitat or in our own backyard.

Unfortunately, the human-animal bond has at times been weakened. Humans have exploited some animal species to the point of extinction.

The Humane Society of the United States makes a difference in the lives of animals here at home and worldwide. The HSUS is dedicated to creating a world where our relationship with animals is guided by compassion. We seek a truly humane society in which animals are respected for their intrinsic value, and where the human-animal bond is strong.

Want to help animals? We have plenty of suggestions. Adopt a pet from a local shelter, join The Humane Society and be a part of our work to help companion animals and wildlife. You will be funding our educational, legislative, investigative and outreach projects in the U.S. and across the globe.

Or perhaps you'd like to make a memorial donation in honor of a pet, friend or relative? You can through our Kindred Spirits program. And if you'd like to contribute in a more structured way, our Planned Giving Office has suggestions about estate planning, annuities, and even gifts of stock that avoid capital gains taxes.

Maybe you have land that you would like to preserve as a lasting habitat for wildlife. Our Wildlife Land Trust can help you. Perhaps the land you want to share is a backyard— that's enough. Our Urban Wildlife Sanctuary Program will show you how to create a habitat for your wild neighbors.

So you see, it's easy to help animals. And The HSUS is here to help.

2100 L Street NW • Washington, DC 20037 • 202-452-1100
www.hsus.org

[[DEDICATION]]

For my family

[[**TABLE OF CONTENTS**]]

Chapter 6: Using a Hosted Wiki Service   131

Chapter 7: Wiki Structureand Ontology   149

Chapter 8: Linking and Categorizing Your Wiki   165

Chapter 9: Wiki Promotion   177

Chapter 13: Things You Can Do With Your Wiki and Where Wikis Are Headed 255

Chapter 14: Resources and Web sites 267

FAQs About Wikis 271

[[FOREWORD]]

Wikis represent one of the most important developments of the Internet era. In its emphasis on user contributions, decentralized decision-making, and collective wisdom, the wiki collaboration model is reshaping the worlds of business, education, and our personal lives. Ultimately, the power of wikis lies not in the specifics of the technology but the way in which they are changing the way we work together, learn, and live our lives.

The Complete Guide to Wikis can help both novices and wiki experts. For novices, it offers a comprehensive overview of the wiki world, touching on both traditional community wikis such as Wikipedia, as well as the increasing prevalence of wiki collaboration in the business world for knowledge bases, documentation, and project management. For experts, it provides specifics on all the different aspects of wiki management, from detailed instructions on structuring your wiki to dealing with the ongoing challenge of wiki maintenance.

Here at PBworks, one of the greatest challenges we face is that our product is often a solution in search of a problem; it is so flexible and has so many capabilities that users may not be sure where to start or how it fits into their business. *The Complete Guide to Wikis* helps the reader build an overall framework for their collaboration strategy and gives enough nitty-gritty to set them on the path to success.

Whether you are a lawyer, designer, teacher, or just a hobbyist, wiki collaboration can make you vastly more productive, and *The Complete Guide to Wikis* can help you achieve your goals.

Chris Yeh, VP Enterprise Marketing, PBworks, Inc.
http://pbworks.com
866-945-4463

Chris Yeh has been building Internet businesses since 1995. He is the VP Enterprise Marketing for PBworks, the world's leading provider of hosted collaboration solutions. PBworks serves more than 50,000 businesses, including one-third of the Fortune 500 companies.

Previously, he was the first investor and interim CEO of Ustream.TV, which provides an open and distributable platform for live, interactive online video. He also helped start numerous other companies, including Symphoniq Corporation, TargetFirst, Juno, and FarSight Financial Services (divisions of D. E. Shaw & Co.).

Chris is an active angel investor and advisor to a wide array of startups ranging from network equipment makers to vertical search engines. He is also the founder and chairman of the Harvard Business School Technology Alumni Association (HBS Tech: **www.hbstech.org**), the co-chair of SD Forum's Startup SIG (**www.sdforum.org**), and the author of the popular blogs Adventures in Capitalism (**http://chrisyeh.blogspot.com**) and Ask The Harvard M.B.A (**www.asktheharvardmba.com**).

Chris earned two degrees from Stanford University and an M.B.A from Harvard Business School, where he was named a Baker Scholar.

PBWORKS

[[INTRODUCTION]]

D espite popular belief, wikis are not as new in the digital age as many people think. Ward Cunningham first introduced wikis in 1995 with WikiWikiWeb. For more than six years, computer programmers who spent their days finding faster and more effective ways to collaborate via the Internet best knew the concept.

As time progressed and technology grew, new methods of using wikis quickly developed. Soon, sites like Wikipedia were hitting the Web and redefining how the Internet was used and what it meant to collaborate on a global scale. Information was no longer controlled by the few who had access to the printing presses — every individual with a desire to share knowledge controlled it.

The modern wiki was born as soon as the first college student logged into a collaborated site to find the birth date of the author they were researching or when a businessman logged in to update his company's profile with their newest products. Of course, wikis are so much more than just encyclopedic sources of information. They are vessels through which organizations, schools, individuals, and millions of others have been able to collaborate on a scale never before seen.

To many the basic concept of a wiki is relatively simple — it is a site on which anyone can add whatever they want to the public record. This is not all-inclusive as a definition for what a wiki truly does though. In reality, a wiki is built on the concept that the whole outweighs its parts. When someone makes a joke about adding an outrageous bit of information to Wikipedia, they do not think about the thousands of individuals who are online at any given time who will see the new addition and delete it.

Like collective intelligence, a well-operated wiki works by making sure every piece is flexible. At any given time, the truth behind a statement or a position on a page can be called into question and restructured to fit the necessary aspects of whoever is reading or writing it.

What this does is create technology that is incredibly simple but has endless applications. The sheer volume of ways in which you can utilize wiki technology to develop a seamlessly integrated wealth of information would have been beyond the scope of imagination only a few decades ago.

In this book, we are not going to simply focus on the 800-pound gorilla in the room, Wikipedia. Rather, we are going to frame the entire concept and technology of the wiki with the means and ways by which a wiki is built and operated. You are going to learn what people are using wikis for, how they were developed, how to edit one, and eventually how to operate one yourself before learning how to take the technology you develop and turn it into a well-oiled, traffic-gathering, information-filtering machine.

Most of all, this book has been written to show this generation and beyond the path by which the world has been moving for nearly two decades — disseminating information over the course of human history into a singular path that works to combine rather than separate. In 200 years, will we still be saying things like, "History is filtered by those who wrote it?" It is a question that not only computer programmers are faced with but also historians, sociologists, politicians, and every man, woman, and child living their life in the midst of a technological revolution.

[[CHAPTER 1]]

The Basics of a Wiki

Wikis are simple in concept. As Jimmy Wales, the founder of Wikipedia, said in 2004, "Imagine a world in which every single person on the planet is given free access to the sum of all human knowledge. That's what we're doing." On the surface, statements like this seem outrageous. It sounds impossible that any Web site, no matter how big the Internet is, could store every piece of information humanity has ever learned.

Upon first visit to any of Wikipedia's 2.9 million English Language articles (as of June 11, 2008), you may find yourself thinking that same thing — there are bits and pieces of information missing here and there that you might point out or notice that others would not. But, here is the genius of the wiki that has made it so viable in the modern culture of faster, sooner, and more efficient: If you find something that is missing or you think should be rewritten, you can correct it.

The winners have always written history. There was never a point in time when the masses were able to record what they saw and collaborate to come to an impartial, collective perspective. Despite criticism that Wikipedia is inherently flawed for this very reason, people, like founder Jimmy Wales, state otherwise, calling it the most accurate encyclopedia in the world and many information resources agree.

If many of the world's past leaders were alive today, there would be thousands if not millions of different perspectives on their lives and what they did during their time. These opinions would litter the Web and would be added, deleted, and revised on Wikipedia. Someone could write their account and someone else could request that the information provided be cited and sourced or corroborated by fellow witnesses. Only when that happened would the information be accepted.

This is the power of a wiki. It does not allow simply anyone to write whatever he or she wants; it allows anyone to question the information that is presented. History has been notoriously slanted toward those who were victorious. Cold, hard facts on the Internet are different, and the course of human history will change because of it.

Defining a Wiki

But, does that truly define in full what a wiki is? Does it define what wikis have done to fundamentally alter the way in which people work and collaborate with one another in the digital age? It cannot. Wikipedia is the best example of what is possible with a wiki, but it is only the tip of the iceberg.

When the word "wiki" was placed in the Oxford Dictionary in 2007, it related it as "a Web site that allows visitors to make changes, contributions, or corrections." This does not mean it has to be useful information or that it even needs to be facts. In fact, when WikiWikiWeb was introduced in 1995, the purpose was to provide a fast authoring tool so publishing could be done quickly via the new technology the Internet provided.

A wiki can be anything you want it to be. Teachers use them to provide their students with updated projects and to keep project resources organized in a single space. Programmers use them for collaborative open source projects on which thousands of individuals may be providing new lines of code at any given time. Businesses use them to manage their projects and ensure new clients are given the same amount of attention as any existing ones. Any way you look at them, wikis are an incredibly powerful resource and one that is going to remain as such for years to come.

Where it All Began

In 1994, Ward Cunningham started programming the first wiki engine. His vision was to create a simple and incredibly easy-to-use online database through which anyone could work. In a time when the programming community was largely built around gathering as much information to oneself as possible and selling the rights to use it, Cunningham was thinking a decade or more ahead of his time — of something in which anyone could access and alter a basic database with ease. He had always worked in the programming and engineering field so for him things were based on logic and function. The simple idea of being able to streamline the sharing of information was so novel and so genius that it made perfect sense to him at the time.

The basis for the name of a wiki is not nearly as technical as many people assume, either. It is as simple as a bus ride that Cunningham took in Honolulu's International Airport on the Wiki Wiki Shuttle — "wiki" being Hawaiian for "fast."

The technical inspiration for the wiki was a bit more pronounced, deriving from the Apple® HyperCard system. The system, which allowed its users to create virtual stacks of cards that supported links among other various cards, was simple and effective. Cunningham simply added the idea that you could comment on and add information to any of the other users' cards. Think of a box full of note cards that is full to its brim. You pull one out and read its contents. If you have something to add you simply write it down and put it back, and someone else can come back later and do the same.

Today, wikis may be the face of collaboration on the Internet, but their most effective uses are in closed environments like schools, businesses, and communities where organizations can put them to use for complex tasks. Monitoring schoolwork, keeping track of memos, or creating plans for when to join up for a bike ride are all ways wikis have become more powerful and more useful.

What a Wiki Does

Cunningham's goal with a wiki was to allow any user anywhere to edit a page or create new content on the wiki using a simple Web browser with no add-ons, no software, and no special knowledge. The goal of the wiki format, though, is through topical associations. This means that on any given page, users can intuitively link between pages by marking up keywords and topics. The software then automatically catalogs and creates a hierarchy of categories from top to bottom.

For example, if a wiki was created for an inter-department memo system and various managers added every memo to the wiki, the software would allow quick and easy methods by which to catalog memos by date, department, and addresses. It would also link things like the signed name of the memo so you could see who had sent how many memos by linking back to that name. Without any additional programming or work, users could then access the root information behind each memo with ease. It would reduce paper use, cut back on cross-checking duplicate memos (for those of you who receive three reminders to fill out the same form from three separate bosses), and much more.

This is the core concept of a wiki in that your contribution may be small, but the moment you publish it, it becomes a part of an intricate web of information that is all dependent and connected with every other piece of information on the wiki.

For good or for bad, when Cunningham created the concept and developed his software, he did not clearly define what a wiki was. As a result, hundreds of different uses for the software and methods of developing a wiki community were developed. In the end though, his original features have been recreated multiple times and have thus become something of a de facto set of definitive terms for any wiki construction:

- Central Location — The files for a wiki need to be centrally located to make it quick and easy to share them and to ensure information is freely available to all users.

- Anyone Can Edit — Anyone can add their information to a wiki without giving up their identity or having an administrator take the job in hand.

- Easy Editing — It should be possible to edit a wiki with a Web browser and no special tools or skill set.

- Simple Formatting — The formatting language behind a wiki should be infinitely simpler than even HTML to allow anyone access to it. For example, it takes an asterisk to create a bullet and a pair of brackets to create a link in a page.

- Lists of Changes — Every page should have a history page to show all recent changes and the course of different edits that have been done on the page.

Of course, it is important to keep in mind that there is no set group of standards for wikis like there is for HTML. While many people are trying to make a standardized way of dealing with this, it has not yet occurred. For this reason, you will need to be sure to read the technical documentation with whatever software you use or whatever wiki you are working with before using any markup (though almost all use the same basic markup methods).

Of course, wikis will always continue to evolve as they have become so much more vital to the language and interaction of the Internet. Here are a few ways that wikis have changed that have made them more vital for use in private enterprises and groups:

- Private Access — Wikis can be run on private servers and Intranets, allowing a number of uses such as administrative work in a business, a school, or hospital.

- Versioning — Storing different versions of a wiki page so that if a major edit comes in, past changes can be reestablished if needed.

- Attached Files — Files can now be attached to a wiki much like an e-mail to provide a more streamlined way of sharing information in a collaborative system.

- Backlinks — Checks all of the pages that link to a single page. This allows you to see how everything connects in a wiki.

- Changes Alerts — When changes are made to pages you have alerts set on, you can log in and see what has been changed. This makes it possible for experts to monitor specific pages (or their own wiki pages for famous people or institutions in Wikipedia) and keep track of what is altered.

- Searching — It is easier and much faster to search wikis with advanced searching technology and spidering used to index pages.

- Printable Pages — The ability to switch the format of a wiki page for printing is new and much easier than it ever was before.

How People Start Wikis

One of the core concepts of a wiki that goes along with their collaborative nature is anyone can start a wiki and therefore anyone can use a wiki. However, this was not the case until 2006. Because wikis were never standardized and because software was often technical in nature, the only way to start your own was to have your own server before getting started.

Most people did not have the skill set or knowledge to build a private server so they could set up a wiki. It was much easier to use it as a visitor than as the administrator. This is a major reason why programmers and engineers almost exclusively used wikis and why standard, everyday applications were few and far between until very recently.

However, in the time it took to develop a more interactive Internet, people started to learn how to develop a better and more effective way to wiki. Hosted wikis were soon a reality and that meant nearly anyone could use the technology behind them for their needs. The only thing you really need to start your own wiki now is a basic knowledge of the core concepts behind a wiki and the markup language used to maintain a wiki.

Sites like JotSpot, Wikispaces, Wikia, and PBworks are great places where people can access nearly all the tools they need to create their own wikis and get started with minimal knowledge. Of course, before anyone starts a wiki, it is a much better idea to get used to the idea of using a wiki by simply adding to an existing wiki. We will get into the details of how to add to a wiki a little more in Chapter 2. For now, let us take a closer look at the various uses for wikis and the one we all know best: Wikipedia.

The Big Kid on the Block — Wikipedia

Everyone knows a little bit about Wikipedia. Whether you used it to finish a college paper or have added to it when you learned something especially interesting, Wikipedia has quickly become one of the largest and most accessed Web sites on the Internet, appearing atop Google™ searches for millions of queries. It is almost impossible to imagine a world now without a resource as vast and detailed as Wikipedia, and yet very few people know what goes on behind this giant and how simple of a process it really takes to create and edit it.

To put Wikipedia's growth in perspective, consider Wales' first project Nupedia, a non-wiki encyclopedia that used heavier, more advanced technology and flopped out of the gate. It did not gather users because the mindset was still very much that information was not free. Encyclopedias, even online, still cost money and needed to be updated constantly. When the project switched over to a wiki and started gaining momentum, it took almost no time for Wikipedia to be born and become the juggernaut of information management it now is.

Wikipedia is a simple resource though. It has the same resources as other wikis, and it does not do anything special or allow any additional uses than what we are used to. It does not build upon old technology to create a new resource or push the boundaries of wikis. It just puts everything in one place and ensures it supports its users by having enough servers and enough space so they can constantly update information — it is a truly collaborative project.

Wikipedia today has more than ten million articles around the world and can be edited by anyone with Internet access. It has been lauded for its accessibility but has been criticized repeatedly for its lack of consistency and the fact that consensus is the key to success instead of expertise on an area of knowledge. Vandalism has been an issue in the past, but for the most part it is a short-lived issue that does not last as often as it seems to.

At the Head of Web 2.0

Since the dawn of the last decade, the Internet has been abuzz with a term that did not have any real meaning until recently — Web 2.0. This term, referring to the second generation of Web development used to create and share content in real time, has come to signify the direction of modern technology. Everything is about functionality, about letting users get in there with sleeves rolled up and truly do something.

Examples of Web 2.0 technology include everything from where users can upload their own videos and share with the vast majority of the world to MySpace where users are free to communicate, share, and discuss anything with anyone from around the world. A behind-the-scenes technical body maintains these sites but users create all of their content. Wikipedia is the epitome of this kind of technology, allowing anyone from anywhere in the world to access, edit, and take part in the process of sharing information.

As one of the forefronts of Web 2.0 along with YouTube and MySpace, Wikipedia has become the face of an entire generation of new technologies and is thus an incredibly popular new way to view the world and to interact with it.

Within Wikipedia's first year it had almost 20,000 articles. By the end of its second year it had 26 language editions, and by the third year it had 46 language additions. Today it has more than 266 languages (as of March 2009) and is the largest encyclopedia ever assembled with more than ten million articles total. The previous record was held by the Yongle Encyclopedia, the work of 2,000 scholars in the Ming Dynasty under the Yongle Emperor in 1407.

However, Wikipedia, as many wiki experts will tell you, is only one of millions of wikis out there, and although it is the most popular and by far the most successful, it is not nearly representative of the myriad ways in which wikis are used. It is not a good place to start using wikis, nor is it a good place to start getting your information about wikis. It is too big and too bulky and much too successful. The scale on which you start talking when you deal with Wikipedia goes above and beyond anything you will ever consider creating for your own purposes. Rather, it is a great example of the sheer volume of potential that a wiki and its format has. When you take into account just how much can be done with a wiki, Wikipedia is the poster child for success.

Adding to a Wiki

Contributing to a wiki is the first step for anyone interested in getting started in the world of wiki management or use. No matter what your goal is for your wiki, you need to first learn how to use the wiki and what will be required of both you and your users when articles are added, edited, or deleted. There are so many different ways to approach a wiki, to build a new set of information, and then to verify that information or entry that you will want to have a firm grasp on the most basic aspects of the process before proceeding with anything additional in the project.

The following information does not apply to only one kind of wiki. This information is designed to be codified for almost any wiki you will find out there. While not every single wiki software and platform is the same as the rest, you will usually find you can build them all together to create a similar situation if you are well versed. To do this effectively you need to be aware of both Wikipedia formatting and the other standards that are present in any wiki editing.

Becoming a Wiki Contributor

The best part about wiki technology is anyone can be a contributor. From the janitor at the local mall to the 13-year-old next to you on the bus, anyone can be editing the wiki you read every day. This means that the task of becoming a contributor is incredibly easy.

To start with, most wikis will make you register. This is not to maintain exclusivity, but to ensure everyone is able to see who edited content and what he or she edited. If a particular user is vandalizing content, this is a safeguard to ensure they can be easily removed from the system and kept from doing anything similar in the future.

After that, you need to be sure you have something to add to the wiki. Do you really know anything that is new or useful to be added to the wiki on which you are hoping to contribute? The vast majority of people are wrapped up in the methods by which they will offer their opinions, but remember that wikis are both unbiased and information based with a consensus method of application. If your peers do not think you are correct, your contributions will be removed.

Having Sources and Citing Them

Along that vein, you need to be sure that anything you ever add to a wiki is done with sources and citations intact. If you have ever seen a wiki page where a marker is placed saying "citation needed" for a particular piece of information, you know that those two little words can make whatever you are reading seem immediately inaccurate and suspect, regardless of whether it actually is or not.

Having citations will not only keep your fellow writers from removing your edits, but will also ensure the changes and contributions you make are maintained and seen as viable sources of information.

In addition to making sure to have citations, you need to learn how to write so you are unbiased. Saying things like "X is the best" will not fly in most wiki formats because the vast majority of wikis are designed to be resources, not opinion platters — those are forums and blogs. Wikis are factual or at least non-partial examples of information distribution. If you know how to maintain your sense of objectivity, you will be much more effective when you add content.

One trick to doing this is looking for any adjectives, verbs, or other descriptions that do not fit inside an academic or educational setting. If you use any words like best, great, useful, bad, or meaningless, you are probably displaying a source of bias. Unless you are sourcing the thoughts of another person and quoting their opinion (the best way to present a dissenting opinion in an academic format), you are probably going against proper wiki formatting.

Where to Contribute

When you are about to start contributing to a wiki, make sure you pick the right place to share your knowledge. The basis of wiki communities is those who contribute have some knowledge or original perspective to add to the core of information that other individuals may not have to provide. This can be the case for any number of people around the globe, but it will not always be the case for you with any given topic.

For example, if you have never played or watched hockey and decide to start contributing to a hockey wiki, your contributions will not be nearly as valuable as they could be compared to other places where you have firsthand knowledge to share. The same will be the case when you start your own wiki. If you want to be as effective as possible and garner attention, you need to write about what you know. Choose a different subject if you are not sure about the one in which you are working — it is good for the wiki and it is good for your state of mind. Always try to enjoy the work you do.

Basic Skills for Wiki Creation

The simplest, most absolute thing you will ever do on a wiki is add a new page. This is the core of all knowledge, the crux from which all content is derived. Until someone creates a page of new content, it does not exist for anyone to edit or add to. Later in this book you will learn about the millions of different ways to use the wiki technology you are gaining access to, but for now you should know that it is going to be incredibly easy to navigate and operate within. However hard you may think working on a wiki is, it is that much easier.

The essential skill set for working on a wiki includes things like navigating that wiki, creating and editing new pages, and linking those pages together. While we will go further into detail on the full tables of markup language for editing and creating wiki pages later in the book, here you will learn the basics of how to use them.

Navigating a Wiki

To start with, remember that all wikis are a little bit different. They all have different aspects and different engines running them because the technology behind wikis has never been standardized. For the most part, most of the wikis you find will be run on services like TWiki, Confluence, or MediaWiki (Wikipedia's base). Generally, even with different engines running behind them, most wikis are relatively the same. If you can use one wiki, you can almost always use another one. You just need to be able to understand what tweaks and differences you will encounter.

To get started, open any given wiki in your Web browser. You will find that most of them are pretty much the same in appearance. You will find a page body that has all the contents of the page listed within it, usually on the right side directly under a headline of sorts. Next, you will find a listing of Webs or sections of the wiki — other words used here might be categories or folders. These are the links on the left side of the page that show what page you are on and what other pages are available or related to your page.

Finally, you will get access to a series of links that show you tools you can use while on that page. These might include links to edit the page, start a new page, or view changes or history of certain pages. For the most part, these links will be at the bottom of the navigation structure after the links that help you navigate the site. This is not always the case, but the links to edit content will always be available.

For the most part, the content on the left side of the page will be split up into categories that correspond to your given wiki. If you are looking at a wiki that is focused on content about a video game for example, the Web categories might be split up for characters, the story behind the game, technical aspects, and various different parts of the game itself. Each would then have a slew of information that delves deeper and deeper into the content related to that category.

Viewing a Single Article

When you click on one single article and view it, you will find that there are quite a few options for you. Visit any given wiki right now and you will find a great deal of options for you to visit and review. Start by reviewing the changes history. Each page will have a changes history that will display all the changes that have been made to the page in question. In a Wikipedia article, you will find three links at the top of the article: discussion, history, and edit this page.

Discussion

The discussion page on any wiki will display any conversations community members are currently holding regarding the content on the page. This is a great place for people to figure out how they want to go forward with some edits and changes to a page. If there are factions in a debate over a particular fact or perspective in an article, there are often ways in which you can discuss these and work them out without having three or four people constantly editing and deleting content on a wiki page.

On the Discussion page, you will often find each section of an article broken down with commentary and questions from various members as certain aspects are discussed to refine a major article. If you have a question or a comment about how an article is written, this is the place to go.

History

The history page will show all of the edits ever made to the article. This can equate to a huge selection of pages and edits going back for years on a site like Wikipedia. An article written in 2001 when Wikipedia went live might have more than 10,000 individual edits on it as the article has evolved — this is especially true for anything to do with current events. For example, the profile of a major politician will often be edited every day by multiple sources, including those of the politician to maintain the message and the facts about their career. If one were to look at the Wikipedia page for George W. Bush, you would find more than 500 edits every 2 months. One can imagine that in the eight years of his presidency, there were tens of thousands of edits to his Wikipedia entry.

This is a great place to go if you want to see if what you are ready to add has already been added or edited. You will be able to find just about every piece of information you need concerning the page you want to edit here.

Edit Page

This is the page where you will go to find and start editing the page. In most cases, this page will consist of a text-editing box where you can list everything that you need to start changing the contents of the page. It will look more or less like a text document, but you will find a slew of different tags in the text that tell the page how to format each bit of text. Below the editable text box, you will find a save page, show preview, and show changes button. Additionally, there might be other tools included from the designer of the wiki such as insert buttons, category changes, and other methods to make changes.

The Sandbox

In addition to the edit page, most wikis will have a sandbox in which you can practice various changes for a page until you get them where you want them. It might take a bit of time to get the right look down for the page. When you do, you can save the sandbox changes you have made and upload them to the wiki where they will go live.

WYSIWYG

There are options on many wikis where you can edit the page in a WYSIWYG mode — this stands for "what you see is what you get." This allows you to make visual changes to the page that alter the basic format and make it easier to adjust how the page will eventually look.

The Actual Edits

You can make basic changes on a page you want to edit by clicking on the edit box and going to the text box where the existing page is located. Remember that almost all wikis require that you first create a profile to login with. This is important because it will ensure that your edits are tracked — this allows the rest of the wiki community to know what was changed and when and who changed it.

While many wikis now offer a WYSIWYG mode for editing, this book will assume that most edits are done in classic text form for a few reasons. First of all, many sites still operate on basic MediaWiki format, which is almost always plain text. Also, it makes it easier to have access to edits on all major wikis. If you come across a wiki that is different than normal ones, it is important that you know what you are able to do on that wiki regardless of the style of edits that are being used.

Again, remember that the following markup is for MediaWiki wikis — other wikis will use different variations of the same markup language. For example, TWiki uses a series of dashes for headings and line breaks that look like " - - - - - " rather than the equal signs that MediaWiki uses "==". To check what your wiki software of choice uses, make sure to check their style guidelines before making any edits. Most wikis will provide a style guide so you know exactly what your edits will look like when you make them.

Additionally, remember that whenever you add new information to a page you need to add references to the page to back up what you just changed or added. If you do not reference a new fact when you add it to the page, you will probably find that someone else quickly deletes it.

To get started, create a blank page on your wiki of choice in sandbox mode. This will allow you to practice with a few different methods of editing and changing the text so you can see what your markup does as you add it and change the text.

Minor Edits

If you decide to make a very small edit to a page, you will need to be sure to mark the spot on the editing page that says "minor edit." This will show that you have only changed a few small things in the article instead of major, significant changes that might show up in a big edit.

Major Edits

If you make major edits, you want to be sure they are done correctly. Simply going in and reformatting an entire article that was already well written is not going to be appreciated by the rest of the community or tolerated for very long. The best way to ensure you do not overlap an edit with someone else is to use the {{Inuse}} tag — place this at the top of the article you are editing and leave it there until you are done editing the page. When you see this tag yourself in an article, make sure not to edit that article until the tag disappears. If someone works on a three-day edit, it can be very confusing for someone else to check out the same page for edits.

Any edit that changes the overall meaning of an article (even if it is only one word) is usually considered major. These should be marked as such so that anyone with an RSS feed on that article can review it and a consensus can be reached on whether the article is correct. Most wikis do not really have much in the way of established guidelines for editing, just suggestions. The best rule of thumb is to always be careful to think of what other editors would think of your changes.

Markup

Below you will find the basic markup language for editing a wiki page. The markup listed is all intended for MediaWiki wikis. The same markup will work on most hosted wikis as well, including Wikia, PBworks, and the rest of the major hosted services. However, some major installed wikis will be slightly different and require a different approach than the rest.

Links and URLs

The basic format for creating a link is to use a pair of brackets that look like "[[text]]". However, there are a few different ways to do this. Let us take the sentence, "Wikis are vital parts of the Internet." In a wiki you want to link as many words as possible to other articles that exist. In this case, you would be able to link "Internet" because it has a major page that relates to the topic. However, you need to be sure that the page you link to is the right page. Here is how you would link it: "Wikis are vital parts of the [[Internet]]."

If you have a multiword link, most wikis will place an under-score automatically in any space. They will usually also capital-ize all lower case words so if the word is lower case in your sen-tence you will be able link to the upper case article within the wiki's database. So, if you were linking to [[world wide web]], the actual link that the wiki follows would look like this: **http://www.yourwiki.com/World_Wide_Web** instead of the text you provided.

Alternately, if you want to link text to a page that is not the exact text, for example, if you wanted to link the word "Internet" to "World Wide Web," you would use the following format: "Wikis are a vital part of the [[World Wide Web | Internet]]." This tells the page that the first part of the link is where to actually go and the second part is what you want to display on the page. You can use this when a word is closely related to an existing article but the exact wording is not the same.

Another important thing to remember with this form of linking is if a word exists for an article such as "nation" and you use the word "nations," you can link to it by using the text [[nation]]s. The markup will automatically make any text attached to the end of the link part of that link. If you want to have text directly con-nected that does not link, you would surround that text with the tags <nowiki> and </nowiki>, calling the HTML to tell the wiki not to link the text.

If you want to link to a page that has parentheses in the page name such as something like Kingdom (Biology), but the text in your wiki article does not have that text, you would simply put the parentheses into the link, such as "[[kingdom (biology)]]" — this would not show the parentheses on your page but would link to the page with them in the title.

Finally, if you link a bit of text to a page that does not yet exist, it will say so when you click on the link and will appear as red in the text. All existing links will be blue. When you click on a non-existing link, most wikis will give you the option to create that page by clicking on the create-a-page button. To create a new page on any wiki, you usually need to be able to link to it from at least one other page first.

When you need to do a redirection from one page to another, the task usually calls for the use of the #REDIRECT command. This will tell the page to redirect whatever the page is to another page. You can also redirect to a specific section of a page with the use of another "#" within the link itself. For example, if you need to redirect from "the Web" to "Internet" but want to go to the "early years" part of the Internet, you would use the following command: #REDIRECT [[Internet#Early_Years]].

While it will not occur in many wikis, there are some situations in which you may want to link to a page in another language. This is usually just the case on major wikis like Wikipedia. But, if you do come across it, you need the language code for that wiki — e.g. [[es:Internet]] would take you to the Spanish page for the Internet.

Categorizing

Putting an article into a category can be a fairly easy process as well. You only need to add the "category" list before the name of the category you would like to use. For example, if you wanted to put an article about wikis into the Internet category, you would use [[Category:Internet]].

Creating External Links

If you want to create an external link, you need to use a single set of brackets and make sure to have them effectively marked within the text. If you simply type a bare URL, you do not need these brackets, but if you want to use them to link a specific word to an external link, you need to use the following format: [http://www.link.com Title]. This will link the external link to the word "title."

Using Images in a Page

To use images within a wiki, you will use another set of commands that are equally simple to master. The following commands are used throughout many different kinds of wikis (based on MediaWiki) to format those images.

The most basic way to include an image in your page is to use the following command: [[Image:image.jpg]]. This will simply call up an image to display in the text. Remember that all images you call must already be uploaded to the wiki. This can be done on most wikis through an additional form.

If you want to add "alt" text to the image, you would use the following format: [[Image:image.jpg|Alternate Text]]. To give an image a caption and have it float on the right side of the page, use the "frame" attribute to push the image off to the side: [[Image:image.jpg|frame|Caption]]. If you want to do the same thing but use a thumbnail size image, replace the word "frame" with "thumb" and the image will be resized to match. If you do not want a caption, use the modifier "right" instead of "frame" or "thumb." Here are a few more commands that will allow you to alter how the image looks on the page:

- Resize the image: [[Image:Image.jpg|50 px]] — always done in pixels.
- Go to the description page of an image — [[:Image:Image.jpg]]
- Link to an image without displaying it — [[:media:image.jpg|Link Text]]

Headings for the Page

Headings will vary within different kinds of wikis, but the most common method of creating and maintaining headings will be accomplished with the use of double sets of ==. You simply add more sets of them for each level of heading you want to create.

- First Level Heading: ==Heading 1==
- Second Level Heading: ===Heading 2===
- Third Level Heading: ====Heading 3====

Basic Formatting

To do basic formatting of the text on the page, you will use the following basic commands in your text:

- Italic Text: ''Italics''
- Bold Text: '''Bold'''
- Bold and Italic Text: '''''Bold and Italic'''''
- Source Code Display: <source language==cpp>SOURCE CODE HERE</source>
- Small Text for Captions: <small>Small Text</small>
- Big Text within Captions: <big>Big Text</big>
- Strike Out Text: <s>Strike Out</s>
- Deleted Material: <del>Deleted Text</del>
- Inserted Material: <ins>Inserted Text</ins>
- Comments in the Page Source: <!−comments - ->
- Subscripting: _{number}
- Superscripting: ^{number}

Special Punctuation:

¿ ¡ § ¶	¿ ¡ § ¶
† ‡ • – —	† ‡ • – —
‹ › « »	‹ › « »
' ' " "	‘ ’ “ ”

Commercial Symbols:

™ © ® ¢ € ¥	™ © ® ¢ € ¥
£ ¤	£ ¤

Mathematical Characters:

∫ ∑ ∏ √ − ± ∞	∫ ∑ ∏ √ − ± ∞
≈ ∝ ≡ ≠ ≤ ≥	≈ ∝ ≡ ≠ ≤ ≥
× · ÷ ∂ ′ ″	× · ÷ ∂ ′ ″
∇ ‰ ° ∴ ℵ ∅	∇ ‰ ° ∴ ℵ ø
∈ ∉ ∩ ∪ ⊂ ⊃ ⊆ ⊇	∈ ∉ ∩ ∪ ⊂ ⊃ ⊆ ⊇
¬ ∧ ∨ ∃ ∀	¬ ∧ ∨ ∃ ∀
⇒ ⇐ ⇑ ⇓ ⇔	⇒ ⇐ ⇑ ⇓ ⇔
→ ↓ ↑ ← ↔	→ ↓ ↑ ← ↔

Other Special Formatting

If you need to show exactly what you type in a wiki, you can do so by telling the page to ignore the formatting with the <nowiki> tag. Anything within this tag will be shown without any wiki markup. It is good for showing how to do markup or simply to ignore the burdens of that entire markup when you start typing.

Additionally, you can tell the page to ignore the wiki markup and not reformat the text while still interpreting special characters with the <pre> tag.

To put in a leading space, a simple additional space on the page to keep the text from being reformatted, you can use a space at the beginning of each line. The page will interpret it accordingly.

Tables of Contents

One of the best things about wikis is that they do most of the things on the page automatically. If you simply create headings in the page, the wiki will automatically generate a table of contents to be displayed. This is a rather simple way of doing it as you can then ensure all your pages are well divided to trigger the automatic table of contents.

Creating Tables

In most wikis, you can choose to either create a table using wiki markup language, or you can use the HTML elements that have been standardized throughout the Web to create them. Because all wikis seem to use different formatting for their tables, we will skip that part for now. However, you will usually find that the tables in your wiki (whether it is one you are creating or one you are adding to) will be set pretty firmly in stone.

Additional Variables (from Wikipedia's Style Guide)

- {{CURRENTWEEK}}   48
- {{CURRENTDOW}}   4
- {{CURRENTMONTH}}   11
- {{CURRENTMONTHNAME}}   November
- {{CURRENTMONTHNAMEGEN}}   November
- {{CURRENTDAY}} 27
- {{CURRENTDAYNAME}} Thursday
- {{CURRENTYEAR}}   2008
- {{CURRENTTIME}}   17:26
- {{NUMBEROFARTICLES}}   2,637,494

- {{NUMBEROFUSERS}}   8,382,898
- {{PAGENAME}}   How to edit a page
- {{NAMESPACE}}   Wikipedia
- {{REVISIONID}}   253637071
- {{localurl:pagename}}   /wiki/Pagename
- {{localurl:Wikipedia:Sandbox | action=edit}}   /w/index.php?title=Wikipedia:Sandbox&action=edit
- {{fullurl:pagename}}   **http://en.wikipedia.org/wiki/ Pagename**
- {{fullurl:pagename | query_string}}   **http://en.wikipedia.org/w/index.php?title=Pagename& query_string**
- {{SERVER}}   **http://en.wikipedia.org**
- {{ns:1}}   Talk
- {{ns:2}}   User
- {{ns:3}}   User talk
- {{ns:4}}   Wikipedia
- {{ns:5}}   Wikipedia talk
- {{ns:6}}   Image
- {{ns:7}}   Image talk
- {{ns:8}}   MediaWiki
- {{ns:9}}   MediaWiki talk
- {{ns:10}}   Template
- {{ns:11}}   Template talk
- {{ns:12}}   Help
- {{ns:13}}   Help talk
- {{ns:14}}   Category
- {{ns:15}}   Category talk
- {{SITENAME}}   Wikipedia

Using Wikipedia

The core philosophy behind Wikipedia is that it operates behind the careful hand of millions of volunteers from around the world. No one is getting paid to contribute their time and knowledge to Wikipedia — they just get to see the contributions they make compiling the largest encyclopedia in the world.

For that matter, every wiki created relies to a certain degree upon the good nature of volunteers. Without people to help put things together, no wiki could operate effectively. They need people to write the pages, edit the poorly written content, and go out to find solid sources.

Your wiki is going to be the same in the end and therefore it is good to get a solid idea of how Wikipedia, the largest of all wikis, works and what you can expect from it when you start putting some solid time into helping with its production.

Editing and Creating Pages on Wikipedia

Beyond the technical aspects of creating and editing pages on Wikipedia (as listed above), there are many different facets to how individuals make use of Wikipedia and what they do when they make their edits. If you want to be one of those few individuals who constantly help create and edit content on the world's largest reference source, you need to know how highly they value content and quality before you do anything of the sort.

To start with, you need to develop a good plan for how you are going to edit content and what it will entail. First of all, you need to be able to remain objective. No original research is allowed on Wikipedia, nor is anything without sources (by default — it will be deleted if you post it).

Wikipedia as a Research Tool

Wikipedia has become one of the foremost research tools in the world for many high school and college students, but there is ample debate about whether this is for the greater good or not. There are too many different ways in which a singular research tool, in which nothing is ever fully verified or confirmed and can be changed at a moment's notice, can be inaccurate.

For this reason, many professors and teachers have banned the use of Wikipedia for any form of formal research. They are largely requiring now that individuals all use a wide variety of different resources for their papers that can be verified in print sources. This is all the more reason why it is important to provide resources and citations for any facts you list in Wikipedia. If a fact cannot be verified with an outside source, it is useless to most of the people using the site. Sure, if someone just wants to know something for a game of Trivial Pursuit or a crossword puzzle what the capital of Eritrea is, they will be fine. But, if they need to know the cause of their second revolution, you would better provide sources.

At the same time, the current push to ban or moderate use of Wikipedia in the classroom is starting to withdraw as more tech-nologically savvy teachers enter the work force. The inaccuracy of Wikipedia is becoming less of an issue, and the maintenance of knowledge by a group of individuals is starting to become a standard in society. People are no longer concerned with the idea of 1,000 people compiling a resource instead of one. Rather, they are worried about who those 1,000 people are.

As the technology develops and knowledge is disseminated more and more freely, these concerns will continue to subside in favor of a more universal, widened approach to knowledge. Until then, be careful how you dictate Wikipedia's use. Teachers should not outright ban it, but should require supporting resources for anything cited from Wikipedia, while students should attempt to still look in print resources and via traditional research materials rather than just refer to the automatic resource that seems to be on the top of everyone's bookmark list these days.

Reliability and General Use of Wikipedia Offline

This brings up the big question about Wikipedia: How reliable is the information printed online and what use does it actually have? There are millions who would cite Wikipedia's ease of dissemination as a perfect example of why it should not be considered a serious resource material. As mentioned above, people cannot create a wiki in this day and age and have everyone believe everything that is listed. It is not in human nature to give credence to popular opinion over the collective intelligence of a population, especially when such a good percentage of that population is willing and able to attack the ideas and pronouncements of their peers.

The debate over whether Wikipedia will be useful for actual research and intellectual pursuits will continue to rage on for years as the site continues to grow and more knowledge is combined into a simple-to-use resource, but the actual question may never be answered as to whether the human mentality can ever truly embrace the idea of intellect by consensus.

[[CHAPTER 2]]

Making Your Own Wiki

Of course, most of you reading this book did not read it so you could learn how to edit Wikipedia. Rather, you probably wanted nothing more than to develop a strategy to build and use your own wiki, either in your work place or for a personal project. For that reason you are going to learn the myriad different ways that the wiki is used and how it is established to build a platform on which to develop your projects.

Whether this is through content wikis that are used for research, hobbies, or documentation, or for process wikis built around businesses and organizations that use wikis for task orientation, education, and productivity, there are dozens of different ways to manage your wiki platform and use it to match your specific needs.

What is Your Wiki About?

Wikis are incredibly popular for a wide variety of reasons. But, before you start putting one together, you need to be able to ask yourself questions about what you will do with your wiki, what you need to accomplish, and how many tasks are present as you create that wiki. To get started, the first question new wiki owners should ask is what their wiki is going to be about. What is it that you want to present to the world in your new wiki and how will you go about doing it?

To get started, you need to start doing research. Unless you are very sure of what you want to do with your wiki, you should constantly be looking around at other wikis. If you are a teacher or business owner and have a good idea of how to use a wiki for your business or job, you will want to start researching how other people have been using wikis themselves. This will allow you to gain a much greater insight into the way the industry works and the myriad uses of the technology that may not have made themselves apparent to you just yet.

The SEO Factor

Another major factor that you will want to consider is if your wiki will be used for public interaction. If you are going to keep it on a private server or intranet and use it for your own devices, then you probably do not need to worry all that much about things like search engines and gaining traffic.

However, if you decide to open your wiki up to the big bad world and let everyone from anywhere in there to edit it, you need to be able to develop a site that can compete with similar sites and other types of Web sites that have keywords like yours.

SEO, or search engine optimization, is the focal point of any good Web site these days as it will determine how high in search rankings your wiki appears depending on what your topics are and what you do to promote it. Luckily for you, wikis are famously good at ranking well in search engines. There are a few good reasons for this. First of all, they are built from the ground up to be friendly to search spiders. They have keywords built into every page in abundance, and they interlink within themselves hundreds of times for ease of use. To top it all off, if your wiki starts to become successful, other people will link to it as a resource of sorts, which will allow you to build and grow your community of users that many more times over as time progresses.

We will not focus all that much on SEO in this book for a few reasons. Wikis are usually great at ranking in search engines, but beyond that, you will probably want to focus more intently on maintaining quality content and control over your users. Beyond that, it can be a bit more frustrating to keep a grip on your site. However, keep in mind that competition is still an issue. Try to find a topic and site that will allow you to compete and you will be that much more successful.

Enjoying Your Topic

Finally, it is important that you enjoy everything you work on. If you choose a topic for your wiki that you could not care less about, it is going to be downright hard to work on it. The research it will take to develop additional information for that wiki will be difficult and can quickly fizzle out. If you are building a wiki for your business or something beyond simply providing encyclopedic information, the goal is to make it a fun project and as accessible as possible to everyone. For example, if you are working on a book with multiple people, you want to ensure the content you choose, the methods you utilize, and the software entailed is something you will all enjoy to keep the process moving along as smoothly as possible.

Content Wikis

The first type of wiki is the most common and the one that this book has been talking about the most thus far — it is the content wiki and it is the one that will ultimately be used to define what a wiki is within the last decade or so. That does not mean this is the only kind of wiki out there but it is the most vital and the most visible so it can be the easiest to create at the same time.

A content wiki might include anything from basic research for a major project to an encyclopedia of information for something like an online game or a hobby. It might be a travel wiki or include documentation for a piece of software that will be updated constantly. Basically, any research- or content-oriented database of information that will need to be updated by multiple people is perfect for the wiki format and is a highly popular way to make a wiki work well within the confines of what has been described in this book thus far.

Examples of Content Wikis

There are hundreds of different content wikis on the Internet — it is by far the most elaborate of any wiki category. Here are a few examples to show you how the technology is being used and in what way:

Wikipedia

Wikipedia is the ultimate content wiki. It was originally created in 2001 after the failed start of Nupedia, a site that was supposed to be an online encyclopedia with a slightly more rigid frame for contributions. The Wikipedia model took off immediately and within less than a decade became the largest encyclopedia in the history of the human race — a sure sign of the times with Web 2.0 tools, wikis, and the digital age itself. Some have called Wikipedia the most accurate encyclopedia ever created while others have repeatedly cited the fact that it is an easily vandalized piece of technology. Either way, the sheer volume of knowledge compiled in Wikipedia by its thousands, if not millions, of volunteers lends itself very well toward a formal definition of what wikis can truly do.

Wiktionary

Piggy backing off the success of Wikipedia, millions of other wikis services have been created that operate in the same way — providing information in an easy-to-operate and easy-to-use format that has defined modern compilations of information. Wiktionary is a great example of this new technology put to use to organize and present a classical information source, the dictionary. This online dictionary has more than 300,000 entries and 400 languages represented in its databases. While most people still refer openly to the Oxford English Dictionary as the primary source of etymological resource on the Internet, the Wiktionary is quickly becoming a representative presentation of almost every language on Earth.

Wikiquote

WikiMedia, the non-profit company that is responsible for Wikipedia, runs both Wiktionary and Wikiquote. Wikiquote is an online encyclopedia of quotations from books, movies, and historical figures in 90 different languages. The database consists of more than 9,000 pages and has thousands upon thousands of different quotes from throughout modern history.

Baseball Reference Bullpen

As an example of the ways in which wikis can simplify an information product that is otherwise entirely too complicated, the Baseball Reference Bullpen compiles more than 38,000 articles on everything you can possibly imagine dealing with baseball into a single resource. This means everything from ballparks, players, major league play, Negro league play, little league, and statistics of every type are all easily cross-referenced in one of the easiest means to read such content on the Internet.

Recipe Wiki

This is a site that takes the common knowledge nature of recipes and takes it to a whole new level with a wiki that compiles cookbooks and recipes from around the world into more than 40,000 different recipes all in one space. It includes articles telling people how to cook certain things, breaking down various types of food groups, and much more.

WikiHow

WikiHow is the world's largest how-to manual. Thousands of volunteers have collaborated since 2005 to write 50,000 how-to articles in six languages that are now read by more than 16 million people a month.

CASE STUDY: BEN GETZ

Ben Getz is an avid fan of the online role-playing game World of Warcraft and has been using wikis for the last two years to help speed through tough parts of the game and research dungeons and character types before taking them on:

"I have been playing online role-playing games for the last ten years or so, since I was in high school, and they have been a major part of my life," Getz said. "Things have come a long way, too. Back in the day, if you did not know how to do something, you hit up a message board, asked a question, and waited around for a few hours until someone was bored enough to answer your question."

"Today, you just go to the wiki," he added. "Right now, I'm still playing World of Warcraft and have been for about three years. Sites like WoWWiki are great because they not only tell you pretty much everything you need to know about your character or a quest, or a profession, but they can be edited right away when changes are made. Back in the '90s if a change was made to a game, it would take players days to figure out how to get around it. Today, it takes about an hour and then everyone has access to that info — it is great."

Wikitravel

Based on the same basic software that operates the world's largest wikis, Wikitravel is a database of more than 14,000 worldwide destinations with information such as the history, climate, landscape, transportation situation, food, and much more for a given area. Visitors add information, and many frequent travelers will attest that Wikitravel is much more accurate than resources like Lonely Planet, which is often updated by a single travel writer once every couple of years.

Other Ideas

These wikis only make up a small handful of the wikis out there that have taken the wiki model and expanded upon it to create a database of information about a given topic. The number of different methods and ways to develop and integrate information has only grown more extensive in the years since Wikipedia was launched and the possibilities are endless as a result.

Process Wikis

The next type of wiki is the kind that will be used more commonly and get less recognition in the digital community. This is the process wiki and it is used more exclusively for things like businesses and organizations with set processes that are better suited for mass collaboration within a wiki database.

This might include everything from project management to task orientation, advocacy, and educational resources for schools and teachers. They are secure wikis that are kept on closed networks where only certain individuals have access to them and are already becoming invaluable tools for millions of professionals around the world in the same way they have been used by engineers and programmers since the mid-1990s.

Project management is easily the single most common use for process-oriented wikis and for that reason, they are usually specialized in ways that makes them better suited to the situation in which you are using them. They are often revamped with tools for tracking things like interviews and research pages. It allows things to be displayed in simple tables that are easier to maintain. These wikis will then be password protected and are used for smaller groups of people within corporations or small companies that need to share information more readily.

Examples of Process Wikis

Process wikis are quickly becoming the most popular way to automate many aspects of projects and utilize more brainpower more effectively in an operation. Here are a few examples of ways that processes can be digitized and streamlined with a wiki:

Weddings

More and more often wedding planners are turning digital, providing every piece of information regarding a wedding on a Web site where those involved can interact easily and quickly. Many brides and grooms are even cutting out the planners and using wikis to control the aspects of their wedding more effortlessly. This allows for an easier gift registry, a faster means to update people about menus, venue changes, dress codes, and dates for certain events. With so much going on in a wedding, and so many people involved, a wiki can speed up the whole process.

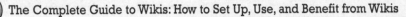

Intellipedia

While you will never be able to see the Intellipedia, you can guarantee that it is one of the more unique and effective uses of wiki technology. Originally implemented after September 11 when U.S. Intelligence agencies were criticized for not sharing information more freely, this technology has been developed to provide a more profoundly simple way for those with the right clearance to provide information about a given topic. Currently, the wiki has more than 30,000 pages and 4,000 registered users sharing information across agency lines to maintain a more effective grasp of the intelligence being providing in the United States.

Ganfyd

This is almost a content wiki in what it sets out to do, but because of how it is used, it is more of a process wiki. Created by doctors and medical professionals in the United Kingdom, the site compiles, compares, and develops medical information, theories, and methods from throughout the medical community in English-speaking nations.

Project Backpack

This is a wiki that is used to help those who were affected by Hurricane Katrina and is a prime example of how a wiki can be altered and implemented for use in ways previously not considered. The site was incredibly successful with more than 50,000 letters and backpacks sent to children in the gulf coast and throughout the country who had relocated.

SourceWatch

This is a wiki that works to provide news and information without any spin — a clear counterpoint to the constant spin-filled news agencies that are being berated with information requests, constant editing, and reforming of the information each day. It follows public information, propaganda, and other information that is often not freely available from political bodies, news agencies, or politicians.

Curriki.org

This site was started by Sun Microsystems and allows teachers and students to distribute curriculum information around the globe freely. It has information and curriculum materials for grades K - 12 and has been used by thousands of individuals around the globe.

CASE STUDY: ELIZABETH SHANKS

Elizabeth Shanks is a seventh-grade teacher at Alderwood Middle School in Lynnwood, Wash. She has been teaching English, Spanish, and history for the last five years, and she has seen a large number of students come and go without allowing themselves the opportunity to be involved.

So, she decided last year after reading an article about wikis in the classroom to give the new technology a shot. Here is what she had to say about their use:

"Wikis are a wonderful tool, and I'm surprised more teachers have not caught on yet," Shanks said. "At first I thought I would need to use something open like Wikipedia. But, I found out there are plenty of software programs out there that let you have login information and limit who can get in. After having all of my students in my Advanced English class sign up, I made them add at least one paragraph a day to a number of different pages I had started (but not added anything to) about the book we were reading. There were pages on themes, characters, plot lines, and all sorts of other things that 12-year-olds tend to ignore in a good story. By the end of the three weeks we spent reading that book, there was more than 40,000 words written by my 23 students on that wiki. They loved it — and I was able to easily and quickly see what they had added. I'll be doing this project again."

Educational Wikis

Collaboration in the classroom has always been a hallmark of the educational system in many countries. The ability to work with your peers and develop ideas in tandem has been vital to how the dissemination of information throughout human history has operated. Without the ability to work in such a small unit of shared knowledge, many individuals will have trouble adjusting to the way in which the world operates when they enter the workforce. For this reason, teachers are drifting more and more toward wikis as a means by which to share curriculum, resources in a class, work in groups (with easy-to-track means of measuring contributions by each student), and plant studies for the students. It is fast, easy, and ensures that all students that are involved can be easily measured.

A single classroom might do this or it might be done by the entire school system to reduce crossover of curriculum and ensure resources available to one class or school are available to all. Wikispaces has become one of the most popular because of its frequent donations of accounts and server space to educational needs.

The Nature of Process Wikis

Process wikis are the epitome of what the technology is about. Teachers, project managers, and wedding planners are among millions of others to utilize modern technology in a way that makes their jobs easier and streamlines the actions of their students, coworkers, or clients. By allowing an organization or group of people to share information dynamically, wikis have become a quintessential tool for building and disseminating information that was always out there and just needed a better avenue to be shared.

CASE STUDY: BRIAN ALK

Brian Alk is a Seattle-area business owner who has been working online for the last three years. He has three employees and a handful of contractors who work for him in short spurts every few weeks. Generally, he used to spend about two to three hours a day keeping track of the projects he was sending out and the work he was getting back along with payments and changes to those projects.

After installing a wiki to his Web server and giving access to all of his employees and his contractors, Alk started seeing a sharp increase in response time and a decrease in the amount of time it was taking him each day to get through all of the content coming and going. After three weeks of having all projects updated to a wiki page and hours with payment information put into an online spreadsheet, he was spending only 45 minutes a day instead of three hours checking that information and making sure it was accurate. By his estimate, he started saving more than $350 a week by not having to do everything manually that could be done by his employees over a wiki.

Community Wikis

The final type of wiki is the one based around a community of individuals who all participate in the same basic activities. This might include a local college's many clubs and student groups or a community-run activist group among many other possibilities. Being able to share resources, gather together, and create easier methods to communicate has made community wikis great tools for any community groups. While many times these wikis become almost content focused, they are founded on the concept of providing access to a full community instead of single individuals.

Community wikis will often feature additional features such as message boards or chat rooms where users can get together and discuss the content they have been adding to the wiki in more direct terms. Ideally, these wikis are not so much about creating a database as much as maintaining relationships.

Examples of Community Wikis

There are dozens of ways community wikis can be utilized to create a high-speed, effective means of connecting with your fellow hobbyists, peers, or friends on the Internet. Here are a few key examples of how this form of wiki is operating in modern society and how it has changed much of what people are doing with their groups and friends.

The Local Wiki

There are cities, small towns, and communities around the world that are starting to turn to wikis as a means to spread their public image, develop a gathering of new residents, and to share information about what they provide in their town (where current hotspots are, where to visit, move, or what to watch out for).

College Wikis

One of the most popular means by which these wikis are being implemented is on college campuses. With thousands of Internet-savvy students that have free time, tend to live their lives between classes, work online, and are eager to meet and share information with their fellow students, it is no surprise that college campuses are very fond of the wiki technology. Campuses like Johns Hopkins University and Ann Arbor (Michigan) are home to two of the bigger community wikis in the country and are regularly being updated with information about student events, the best places to eat, salons, textbook deals, and everything else you might need to stay alive long enough to get that long, sought-after degree.

Entertainment Wikis

On the flip side of the community wiki is the entertainment wiki, a resource that allows individuals to combine the basis of a content wiki with the interaction and familial relationship of a community wiki. There are thousands of these wikis and they tend to be even more fully developed than the most complex content wikis due to the rabid interest of their fan bases.

The Marvel Comics Database, Wookieepedia, WoWWiki, and many more are great examples of sites that have been maintained by legions of fans of Marvel Comics, Star Wars, and World of Warcraft respectively. They build surprisingly complete databases about nearly everything to do with each category of entertainment.

Other popular entertainment wikis you might hear about include the Memory Alpha (a Star Trek wiki), LyricWiki (a complete database of song lyrics), Lostpedia (dedicated to the hit show co-created by J.J. Abrams), and many more on just about any major topic you can imagine.

CASE STUDY: MHIYANG NGUYEN

Mhiyang Nguyen started a wiki early last year to help maintain track of the students involved in her newly formed club at the University of Washington. The club was devoted to cycling in and around the Pacific Northwest, and while there were already a few clubs doing the same thing, she wanted to make it more organic and easier for students to join up rather than constantly having to organize large group outings.

"We did not want to need to have a dozen people out there at any given time for each ride we went on," Nguyen said. "We wanted it to be easier to put together so that I wouldn't need to be involved with every ride. We were not an official club with the school yet either so we did not have resources like e-mail access or a Web site. My brother is a whiz with this kind of stuff so he asked if I wanted to put up a wiki."

"We went ahead and did it and the response was tremendous," she continued. "Everyone was able to logon and create new rides without having to consult me. They could update weather information for each other, list things they needed for food or drinks, and have chats about routes. In two months we had about ten rides a month and last month we hit a new record with 24 rides, only four of them put together by myself. It is been great and everyone is loving the wiki."

Other Forms of Wikis

There are of course hundreds of other different forms of wikis out there that have been garnering more and more interest as the technology evolves. There are new formats for everything from providing recipes to creating original article content for a Web site. Guilds in online gaming use wikis to promote their various events while offline groups such as kayakers or rock climbers will use wikis to display the best new places to visit in a given time of the year.

If you are looking for wikis that are currently existing, you should visit one of the following lists of wikis to learn more about the sheer volume of wikis and what they provide currently on the Internet:

- **http://en.wikipedia.org/wiki/List_of_wikis** — This is a complete list of every wiki currently entered into Wikipedia organized by size
- **http://meta.wikimedia.org/wiki/list_of_largest_wikis** — A database of the largest wikis in the world as maintained by WikiMedia, the largest supplier of wikis
- **www.wikiindex.org** — A wiki dedicated to wiki indexing with more detailed information about each entry

Researching Content for Your Wiki

Each type of wiki will involve a different process for getting updated with the newest information. A content wiki, for example, will rely heavily on the knowledge base of its users along with the consensus of other users. A wiki that shares information about a popular online game might have more than a dozen users who have all accomplished the same feat in the game. Each user will then log onto the wiki and attempt to add just a little more detail about what the feat entails, providing the most complete and detailed description available about that feat, all gathered from real players.

One person might first describe a boss they defeated in the game. The next person might come along and describe a strategy they used with their given character. Another person might describe their own strategy and so on until there are detailed descriptions of the boss along with ten different viable strategies for defeating them. And of course, if the strategies are not accurate, other users can always access the wiki and say that the strategies were not nearly as accurate and a consensus of the group can be taken to decide whether this is the case or not.

In the end, the best form of research for most wikis is going to be personal experience. While sites like Wikipedia frown upon original research, most wikis — especially if they are your own — must rely on that original experience to create a consensus report on content. If you need details on the best places to rock climb in Utah in July, you need people who have been out to the various cliffs and have climbed them to report what they have seen, where the conditions are best, and where the rocks might be a bit too loose for safety. This kind of connection can make it possible for instant updates from around the state on rock climbing conditions so that you never have to wonder if you will find a good wall when you head out on a given Saturday afternoon.

Research starts with your users, but it does not necessarily end there. At any given time you might find that the content on a wiki is inaccurate and the users on it are content to let it remain inaccurate. In these situations it is important to institute things like source citing. Most wikis require a specific source to be cited for any given piece of information. With a wide-open framework where anyone can edit anything, it can be frustrating if someone gets into your wiki and changes content without providing backing sources.

To combat this, many people will simply refuse to put up content without a specific framework by which to manage a lack of resources. This means that anything without resources would be deleted and two other members must verify all of the edits. The method of research control is important to be sure that your wiki maintains its viability in the field it exists.

In the case of a process wiki within your work place or on a closed network, research is a different matter altogether. Usually these kinds of wikis are maintained by keeping things simple. You need to have administrative access to things to make master edits, lock down certain articles, and to be sure that content cannot be continuously altered when it is not something that will be updated; for example, lesson plans or assembly plans for an elementary school or content that only a handful of people in the administration of that school would need to alter, and after a certain date, the alterations would be minimal.

Finding Collaborators to Help with Your Wiki

When you first start a new wiki, you need to have people on hand who can help you get it started. Without a few good hands to help you create, edit, and monitor content, it can be hard to get started. This is especially true for content wikis that rely so heavily on producing large sums of content as fast as possible. Without that content, you are going to find that it is a bit too hard to get people to visit your site. You need a reason why your resource is better than the rest and that means you need starting points.

Many new content wiki owners will pay people to produce content while others will recruit friends in a group or simply stay up late a few weeks straight developing their content. It is a tough road to being a fully successful wiki without a crew of solid assistants to produce and maintain content.

Content Wiki Recruitment

We are going to separate the three different kinds of wikis because the only kind of wiki that is going to have a real problem getting the contributions it needs are content wikis. These wikis are going to be bare and empty when you first start them. You might be lucky to have time to write 25-50 pages a week yourself. If you are working in a major field, you might require as many as 2,000 or more articles to be a viable source of information and that can make it very hard to get started.

When you first start your wiki, find friends and family who can help. You need to have a good 200 or more pages of content that is interconnected with itself before you start doing anything else. There are two reasons for this. First of all, you need to perform effectively in SEO by having as many pages out there as possible. The more people that see the site, the more of them you can get on board.

Second, you need to show that you are as dedicated to the wiki as you expect your contributors to be. No one wants to produce content for a site when the owner of that site does not want to do so themselves.

While we will go more into detail later on how to promote a new site, let us take a look at a few more detailed aspects of what goes into a new content wiki's first contributions.

Process and Community Wiki Management

Contributions for a process or community wiki are completely different than those you might see in a content wiki. Instead of having to recruit and compile a group of intelligent individuals who can proffer their knowledge on any number of topics, you need to maintain a steady flow of information and balance in your wiki. The problem with having unlimited contributors is they all have different brains and different perspectives. It is all too easy to allow those perspectives to clash and ultimately create a series of different conflicts. Of course, the nature of these conflicts will always shift as different takes on different issues arise, but the core concept will always be there. No two people will ever 100 percent agree on a subject.

To maintain the issues that undoubtedly arise when two people disagree on a wiki, put in place safeguards within process and community wikis that allow you to ensure a safe, well-moderated interface between individuals. You do not want people openly yelling at each other whenever they disagree (especially in a classroom setting) and you do not want to negate the value of an open forum by censuring people's right to discuss points of disagreement. Limit access to certain pages where needed with passwords and Web specific users and always maintain a valuable, heightened sense of awareness, either by yourself or through a moderator. Moderators can watch what is happening on the wiki and ensure no one gets carried away with themselves and their opinions.

Conclusion

The goal of a wiki is to find a new way to bring together a confluence of individuals who are equally interested in a given topic. For this reason, you are going to find hundreds upon hundreds of potential uses for wikis on the Internet. This is great news for anyone that is creative enough to find a new way to use existing technology and even better news for those who simply want to build on what others have done in the past. However a wiki is used, it is in the spirit of collaboration and free sharing of knowledge that has brought it this far. Communities, content databases, and organizations looking to speed up various processes are all going to benefit immensely both now and in the years to come.

CASE STUDY: STEFAN WILLIAMSON

Stefan Williamson started working for the Wikipedia editorial staff (volunteer corps) in 2005 and has been an avid worker in their midst for the past four years, keeping track of more than 200 articles directly and regularly logging into the Web site to check for recent additions, changes, and deletions to make sure no one has been overly brash with their changes. He has this to say about the risk of vandalism:

"I was really surprised when I first started," Williamson said. "I thought for sure there would be more issues with vandalism on the pages than what I usually see. Of course, there are plenty of problems regularly, but there is this shared sense of ownership and control that so many people have that whenever there is a problem, it is fixed within seconds. Someone sees it and someone fixes it right away."

"The biggest (and funniest) problem I can remember is when Stephen Colbert started asking his viewers to make edits to pages on Wikipedia," he added. "They were doing it for weeks. I wasn't working on those pages, but I saw how many edits and rollbacks went through them. It was a bit of a headache, but with this many people taking ownership and control over the info, things just do not stay wrong for very long."

CHAPTER 3

The Technical Side
of Wikis

Upon deciding what you will be doing with your wiki and how it will be formatted and developed, you need to start getting involved in the more technical aspect of the process. This means things like where and how you will host your wiki (or if you will use a hosted service). You will learn which software options are available for those who decide to host their own wiki and what you will need to know about wiki markup for use in these situations. Formatting, HTML use, and page modes are all vital here and without the right construction, your wiki can quickly devolve into a mess when you open it up and start letting people dig.

Hosting Your Wiki

When you start creating your own wiki, the first thing you need to decide is where and how your wiki will appear on the Internet. Are you going to host it yourself on a server where you will be responsible for all the maintenance, or are you going to have someone else host it for you, keeping backups and maintaining the service each month on your behalf? The difference between the two is not as great as you might think, but in the end, it will depend on what kind of service and style of management you are most comfortable with.

Hosted Wiki Services

The first of the two options is to go the easy route — having a hosted wiki service take care of the technical stuff for you. This is generally the preferred route for all small wikis and content/ community wikis. You will probably need to go with a hosted service if you want to work on a closed network, but if you are simply sharing information with your peers in a given field, you will need to find a good way to present it — hosted services are a good way to do this.

A hosted wiki service will offer a few things. First of all, it makes it much easier to interact with different parts of your site. It can be hard to develop your own infrastructure for the site, including things like where you will post your wiki, how you will submit it to search engines, and how you will control your contributions and maintain the quality of the wiki. While installed wikis are often do-it-yourself to the extreme, hosted wikis will allow you to maintain these things from easy to use control panels; much in the same way a site like Blogger or Wordpress allows you to maintain your blog and its comments much easier. You will ultimately sacrifice control for ease of use.

It is still possible to post your wiki under a domain name of your choosing and make it generally look the same in every way and form as any other standard wiki, but you will be hosting it with a free service that allows you to start much smaller. This is the best choice for nearly anyone that is just getting started with an online wiki and needs the small scale and free form of a hosting service.

Factors to Consider in Your Hosted Service

When looking for a service under which to host your wiki, you need to keep a few select things in mind. Here are a few considerations before uploading your new wiki:

- Setup Ease — Every now and then a wiki is created for a quick and easy process. Maybe you are going on a trip for the weekend or need to coordinate gift giving for a wedding (this is the 21st century's answer to the gift registry). You do not want to spend hours formatting a wiki that is only going to be used by a few people for a couple weeks though. Fast and easy setup can make this much easier for numerous situations.

- User Invites and Limits — If you think you might attract hundreds of users to your site, you will need to be sure the hosted service can handle all of those accounts. Many times, wikis start to cost more money if you have more than a handful of users, so checking this first is a must for large-scale projects.

- Storage Space — You need to be sure that your storage space is sufficient. If you think you are going to be charged additionally for the storage that you need to effectively run your wiki, you need to look for a better option or resign yourself to paying.

- Private wikis — If you want to have a private wiki for only your friends, you need to be able to do so without paying extra; some free services will charge you to do this.

- Protect Your Pages — Some hosted services will not allow you to ensure the security and protection of your pages. You need to be able to protect pages on an individual basis. Select which ones you want to be able to protect and do so effectively.

- Cost of the Wiki — What will your hosted service cost? Most services offer some form of free service, but how much will you actually get for that free account? Usually, not all that much. Know what you want and check to see what you are going to be giving up for lesser costs — many times it will be advertising of some sort.

- How Many Can You Have? — If you plan on creating four or five wikis, you may want to double check and see if your hosted service is going to be able to accommodate your plans. Many times this will put you into a higher cost bracket than simply getting a hosted account from a regular hosting company and uploading your own software.

- Exporting Data — Wikis are databases in the strictest sense of the word. You need to be able to access and move that data on a whim. Make sure the service you use will allow you to do this when you decide you are going to do so.

Generally speaking, the above criteria are not going to break down the wiki options into any discernable categories that tell you which ones are best and which ones to avoid. It is too hard to make such a blanket statement. This is the fastest way to get your wiki up and running, but to be sure that you make the right choice and do not get stuck with an unmovable, overpriced wiki in the future, here are a few details about the options that are out there.

The Options

There are dozens of different options out there for who can host your wiki. However, there are a few that are more popular than others for a variety of reasons. Here are the top hosted wiki services and what they offer that others do not. Do not assume that because a service you use or have heard of in a good light is not listed it is not a good service. There are dozens of amazing services out there that are coming up every day. These are just some of the best observed by this author.

Central Desktop

This service allows you to create a hosted wiki and then go above and beyond the basics of that wiki with a whole slew of basic collaborative features that make them very popular. Included are features for project management, calendars, discussions, and of course wikis. You can create two workspaces and have five users for free or can pay $25 a month for up to ten users (there are plans for higher after this).

Cospire

This is a site that allows you to use both blogs and wikis with a built-in categorization feature to develop a community style interface. All aspects of the site are free, much like a social network or blogging host because of advertisements.

EditMe

This will allow you to build Web sites in the basic wiki format. Essentially, the site has tools for access control, blogging, and WYSIWYG Web site creation. The basic cost is $4.95/month and will go higher from there to match the features that you add to your account.

JotSpot

This is a company that was originally created in the early 2000s and used as a wiki application company and was later purchased by Google in 2006. The site allows you to add functions to your wikis with things like applications, documents, spreadsheets, calendars, and photo sharing through wiki technology.

PBworks

This is one of the premier hosted services for wiki creation and has been around for quite a while. The tag line is you can create a wiki as easily as a peanut butter sandwich, and the site is not too far off in their assertion. It is incredibly easy and free to get started, with upgrade options including $99/year for teachers, $8/user/month for businesses, and $499/year for premium community wikis.

Socialtext

This service provides a base for enterprising wikis. The goal here is to allow things that are central to business operations such as e-mail integration, blog publishing, file management, and other corporate desktop activities.

Wikia

Created by Jimmy Wales, one of the cofounders of Wikipedia, the goal of this MediaWiki-based service is to provide easy-to-create wiki tools for anyone who wants to create their own wiki. Generally, this is not for personal wikis, but many large-scale content wikis have been started on Wikia.

Wikispaces

This service is an incredibly easy to use and highly popular option for those looking to start their own wiki, much like Blogger does for those who want to create a blog for the first time. The primary user of this service tends to be the educational community with free accounts available to get started and upgrades available for premium offerings with more storage and users.

Breaking Down Your Options

For the most part, the wikis above will allow nearly anyone who wants to create a wiki to be able to find a service that works well for them and put together their wiki. However, there are some things that you might want to consider. For example, if your primary goal was to have ease of use in the wiki, your best bets are going to be EditMe, PBworks, or Wikispaces because they are designed for anyone to use easily without needing to learn much about the finer details.

For those seeking a good solution for their community wiki, you want to look for something that is easy to use and has tools that allow e-mail integration, invitations, calendar use, and other community-focused tools. Wiki services like PBworks, Wikispaces, and JotSpot are all good for this kind of service.

For process-focused wikis, it is vital to have a good balance of function and form. While other wikis need things that are easy to use, process wikis need to be able to manage tabular data and contain databases of information more easily than a standard wiki probably could. Spreadsheets and e-mail notification are vital while integration of calendars, word processing, and other basic corporate desktop tools are very important as well. Good examples here are Central Desktop, Socialtext, and JotSpot.

Finally, content-focused wikis are all about scale. You want to get as many users to add as much content as possible. The more active your wiki writing community is for a content wiki, the more successful that wiki will be when it gets to the larger scale. Additionally, you need to be able to do things like upload photos, change management, allow discussions, and rollback vandalized pages. The best services for this include Wikia, Cospire, Wikispaces, and PBworks.

Creating Your Own Host

The other option, and one that anyone serious about a large-scale wiki should consider, is to create their own wiki on their own server or virtual server. This method requires quite a bit more technical know-how, but allows you a much greater amount of control over how the wiki will be presented and how it will operate for you in the course of its lifespan. Generally for this method you will use an open source software platform that will be installed on your server of choice where you can control all the things that a hosted wiki would normally control for you. It is the ultimate way to build your wiki but it can be a lot harder than other options out there.

Choosing the Right Wiki Engine

Wikis engines are the software programs that will run on a Web server of your own choosing where it will allow your users to create, edit, and publish wiki pages. When you use any wiki, you are using it through the wiki engine that the site's owners and operators designed. When it comes time to choose a wiki, many times a hosted service that is filtered through multiple servers has too few resources and does not provide the options you specifically know you need. If these will not be enough, that is when you need to start looking for your own wiki engine to install on a server and operate solo.

It is hard to make a choice about software though. There are so many options out there and without a preset designation for wiki markup formatting, they all operate a bit differently. Some people choose to go with what they know and pick up WikiMedia, the basis for Wikipedia, while others choose something else.

The Different Kinds of Wiki Engines

There are many different basic kinds of wiki groups out there. Each category has different requirements from its users and different solutions for their problems. With more than 50 engines on the market and dozens more on the way, it is no surprise that many people find it so hard to make just one choice. You are going to need to figure out the capabilities of the engines you need, the requirements of your particular wiki, and then compare the two to make the right choice for your wiki.

Luckily, money is less of an issue with this decision. Because wikis are part of the Web 2.0 evolution of software, their engines are almost always open source. This means that most wikis will operate without needing you to pay any money for them. People work on the software in their own time collaboratively and compile it with no credits and free access to everyone.

Of course, with open source software comes all the problems attached and you will get minimal direct support for it. Usually you can find message boards and fellow users who can help you out, but do not expect much in the way of resources from a governing body on the engine you choose. Also, if you want to have help with installation, upgrades, or changes to the software, you are almost always on your own (and upgrades often come with open source software).

The Five Kinds of Wiki Engines

Before selecting a single type of wiki engine to operate your wiki with, let us take a look at the five different kinds that are out there and what they each entail for your needs.

Desktop Wiki Engines

These will allow you to run on your computer when they are not accessible to anyone else. They are not connected to the Internet and are generally used simply for keeping track of your files and to do lists. They are great ways to organize your work without spending hours formulating an archaic file-stacking method and they are perfect for note taking. Examples like TiddlyWiki operate by creating a wiki with Java in a Web browser while offline for you to use within the confines of your own computer.

Hosted Consumer Wiki Engines

This type of wiki is made with the goal of being as easy to use as possible. These wikis are generally hosted and much easier to use than open source software, but that means they are lacking in customization and control over user access, appearance, and their size and accessibility. For those that want a very basic, easy-to-use wiki, this may be your answer.

Industrial Wiki Engines

These are for open source engines that will allow you to do just about everything you need with a wiki. They will include all the newest security features of wikis, document creation, spam protection, and everything else you need to maintain a wiki that is free of all the modern problems that so many Web sites and online software programs have. Examples like MediaWiki are designed to provide the backbone for the largest and most complex wikis in the world, including the likes of Wikipedia, Google, and Motorola. You need your own server for these programs, and you need to know a bit about installing and maintaining software on a server.

Specific Use Wiki Engines

There are some wiki engines that are designed for one specific task, whether it is for e-mail management, writing a book, publication of documents, or content management. These wikis will also require that you have server access and know how to install complex open source software on your own.

Development Wiki Engines

The last category of wiki engines will include anything that is used for specific development projects. There are services like TWiki that allow for the inclusion of dozens of different plug-ins that all work in tandem for easy upgrade and access for anyone working in the development of software, ideas, or project management. They will usually allow you to expand basic wiki functions in any way you want. These engines are for those who have complex, major projects, usually programming or engineering related, and need an organized space in which to work on them.

What You Need in a Wiki

While it is useful to know what is available in the wiki engines currently on the market, it is even more important to have a clear idea of what you will need from your own wiki engine. If you do not take the time to figure out what your wiki will require, it will be hard to figure out what requirements you might need two, three, or even six months down the line.

The Skill Level

Who will be using your wiki? If they are going to be computer engineers, you can assume that they know how to use just about anything you put in front of them (or at least figure it out). However, if they are stay at home moms who are adding their home-grown recipes to a database, you will need to be sure you target their specific skill set and knowledge base. Basically, you should ask yourself if they already know how to use basic computer software on a daily basis. Will it be tough for them to log into your wiki and add content, or will you need to create a WYSIWYG type of wiki that is easy to edit in the same way that a word processor is easy to use on a desktop?

The best way to do this though is not to just guess what new users might be able to do. You should find a new user (a friend or family member) and have them sit down in front of examples of each wiki engine and see if they can use it. If they have trouble editing or adding to Wikipedia, you may want to find a slightly easier to use method.

The Volume of Users

The second thing to consider in your wiki is just how many people will be using it. If you set up a wiki and expect there to be only four or five users, you can almost get away with a hosted wiki. But, if you are aiming for a worldwide community of contributors and thousands of new pages of content in the next few months, you are going to need a platform and wiki engine that can support that volume.

Your Visitors

Third, how many people will there be visiting your wiki? If you expect a handful of people in a local process wiki, you probably do not need to worry all that much about scalability. But, if you think you might have 10,000 visitors a month within six months, you had better have an engine in place (and a server) that can handle that kind of traffic. You need to have tools that can work well with a small number of users and then scale to support a much higher volume in future months or years. For the most part you can figure these things out simply by seeing what each wiki engine is capable of. For example, WikiMedia is clearly a scalable engine as it runs the world's largest wikis like Wikipedia.

Security

Security is vital for some wikis. If you are going to be sharing important information with your fellow users, you better have a means of controlling and protecting that information. However, if you think your wiki is going to be purely entertainment and need not be too concerned with counteracting vandalism or security breaks on your server, you can afford to be a bit more lax.

Automation

Automation is one of those things that has sped up countless processes in the world via digital means. Being able to have a software program quickly and easily create a table with information you have provided makes life much easier when you are dealing with large volumes of information. Things like e-mail notification to see when changes are made to certain pages or being able to send notes in to be updated into a wiki page automatically are features that can be very helpful, especially for those constantly on the go who need absolute control over their wiki. There are dozens of different applications and add-ons for some wiki engines if you know where to look for them.

Your Expertise

Of course, if you find your needs call for one of the more complex wiki engines on the market but you do not really have the knowledge you need to use it, you had better rethink your decision or find someone who can help you out a little bit. Consumer level wiki engines are made for ease of use while development wiki engines are for those who can figure out the nuts and bolts and use them to their advantage. Do not over extend yourself or you will spend more time figuring out your software than you will building the wiki.

Making Your Decision

It is finally time to figure out which wiki engine you are going to use for your wiki. While you can go much deeper into the details of your decision (and should if you have the technical know-how to do so), here are a few quick shortcuts to figuring out which wiki is going to be best for your needs.

If you will be publishing content, creating content, or working with a content focused wiki, your best bets are with MediaWiki or DokuWiki. If you are working on advanced applications or content management, your best option is TWiki because of its expandability. If you will be using your wiki in a business, your best bet is Socialtext. And finally, if you will be using a wiki to have fun, you should work with TiddlyWiki because of its options and ability to download and use the wiki offline.

The Options

There are dozens of wiki engines out there. However, here are a few of the most popular and what you can expect from them when making your choice:

XWiki

XWiki is a big wiki engine that will work for large-scale wikis for nearly any use. It is a commercial, open source wiki, which makes it a bit odd in application. The company created their software open source and sells implementation and scaling services to make money. You can either use their software on your own or pay them to help you implement it.

It comes with user authentication for security on every page along with full WYSIWYG editing. However, pages must be edited as a whole (no small section editing like on Wikipedia) and it allows you to create PDFs from pages with ease – a great tool. It is a tough installation on your own because of the software's complexities, so you may want to consider finding help or educating yourself a bit more fully when implementing this wiki engine.

TWiki

One of the more commonly used wiki engines out there, TWiki is known for its ability to easily extend and add functionality that you might need for your specific project (it has more than 300 plug-ins). It also has professional services to go with the open source nature of the software and can be used for nearly anything if you have the imagination for it.

Security wise, this wiki engine allows you to control the access, editing, and implementation of content throughout the wiki. You can restrict access based on groups and other basic bits and pieces and the wiki can be edited via markup language or WYSIWYG mode. You can also edit sections natively or upgrade with plug-ins for more direct control of your edits. PDF creation is possible with add-ons as well and installation is pretty simple. You will not need a database as it is run on Perl, but you will need a few other server-side installations to make it run.

MediaWiki

The big dog out there is MediaWiki, if only because of the exposure it has gotten as the engine behind wikis like Wikipedia and Wiktionary. It is the biggest and probably best publishing platform around for ease of use, scalability, and overall speed but is light in things like security if you need your wiki in a secure, corporate environment.

Included are highly useful editing tools, including but not limited to WYSIWYG editing. You can easily edit sections of a page and can create PDFs of any page as you edit. Installation is easy but requires MySQL database creation on your server. Because it is written PHP and OCaml, the software can be a bit of a pain to maintain, but if you have a basic understanding of databases, you should be okay in installation.

DokuWiki

DokuWiki is a very simple wiki platform that removes many of the high-end features that people need in favor of an easy to use, simplistic platform. It is open source and very bare bones but it works well and is scalable to a decent degree. For those with limited technical knowledge and a need for a server-side wiki engine, this is often a good choice to go with. Wiki markup is simplified with button integration for certain tools and most of the pages and editing sections are easy to understand and implement. Pages are all stored in text files that make it easier to install and implement but might limit what you can do with them in terms of search and plug-in or application integration.

Generally, expect a fast, easy to use platform that provides minimal extra features with DokuWiki. If you want more features, you will definitely want to go with MediaWiki or TWiki, but if you only need basic wiki functionality, this is a great way to go.

Formatting and Design

The basics of a wiki are simple. You want it to look neat and clean and be easy to navigate. If it takes a user too long to access what they need from your wiki or your page is a big mess of text, you might waste the valuable traffic you get or lose interest from your users. This is why so much wiki markup language is based around hierarchies and careful implementation of headings, links, and categories.

We have already gone through the various markup that is included in most wikis, but you will also need to know how these are implemented.

Page Structure

Pages are created with sections headers and a table of contents in mind. Often, a page that is bare bones without enough content to provide headings or a table of contents can be integrated into another page or flat out deleted. So, it is important that pages have enough information to warrant their existence.

Headings are your primary means of creating a hierarchy and are also vital for things like search engine optimization. In a page, you will use at least two or three different primary headings and possible secondary or tertiary headings to break down the content.

The page might look something like this when you complete it:

```
Content Introduction
==Heading 1==
Content Section 1
==Heading 2==
Content Section 2
===Subheading 2.1===
===Subheading 2.2===
==Heading 3==
Content Section 3
==Links==
*[link]
*[link]
```

This is clearly a very simplified look at a wiki page, but if you go to Wikipedia and look at any given page in the database of articles, you will find something that looks very similar to this format. Pages start with a 200- to 400-word introduction, and then break up the rest of the content into smaller sections that are easier to read and to edit. This is vital to make your job a bit easier when editing content as well because you will then be able to just click on the "edit" link next to a subheading.

Using bulleted lists and tables are vital aspects of successful wiki formatting. You need to be able to create content that is easy to follow and digest. Each cell is separated by a single vertical break (or pipe) and will look something like this:

```
| *column one* | *column two* | *column three* |
| content here | content here | content here |
```

This would create a table that looks like this:

Column One	Column Two	Column Three
Content Here	Content Here	Content Here

There are additional modifiers you can use to change the color of the table boxes, the text size, and links within those cells. But, for the most part, this is the most basic way to create a table and it is highly recommended that such things are used in your wiki to break up content more effectively.

Layout Formatting Using HTML

While wikis have been designed to be much simpler than Web sites by using a simplified markup language in the place of HTML, you will need to use HTML to control the basic layout and formatting of some aspects of your page. This is not the case when you use a hosted service or a WYSIWYG editor, but with many self-hosted wiki engines you will need to get in and finely tune the nuts and bolts on your own if you want to make any significant changes.

The left hand bar on most wikis with the navigation links is controlled with HTML and you can usually integrate HTML tags into the wiki text markup to make certain changes that are not otherwise supported, such as strikethroughs or telling the page not to read the wiki markup (<nowiki>). This is a basic method of extending the functionality of the wiki without having to make any major changes to anything.

It is impossible to explain in full how HTML operates within a book about wikis, but you can find a great deal of detailed information about how HTML works and how it is used in wikis throughout the Internet and usually within the documentation for the wiki engine or hosting service that you are using, as it is a common addition to functionality.

Conclusion

Wikis are probably one of the most versatile new technologies on the Internet and at the same time they also happen to be one of the least standardized. There are dozens of ways to do any one given thing and people are constantly developing new and differing ways to alter or rethink those methods. If you want to be effective with your own wiki, you need to think about what it needs to do, how it needs to do it, and ultimately how much time and effort you are willing to put into making those things happen. If you do not have the resources for a complex, code-based wiki, a hosted solution may be the best option for you. If you only need a small resource for a handful of individuals, a big platform may not be the best bet, and if you are looking for something easy to use for your users, you may want to steer clear of anything that lacks clear guidance and a basic method of documentation and tutorial.

Wikis are only going to continue growing in use and in due time, one imagines that the language and formatting will be further standardized. But for now, work with what does the job best for you and ensure you are creating a valuable resource that produces more than it consumes from you in terms of energy.

[[CHAPTER 4]]

Wikis for Businesses

A business is a carefully managed entity that requires a great deal of organization to be an effective money making machine. To that end, if you want to use a wiki to help streamline some of those processes, you need to start considering ways in which you will actually make things easier and more effective.

Benefits of a Wiki

A wiki is going to be a tremendously beneficial system for implementation within a business structure, but just how much benefit is a company likely to get from such a system? Compared to existing collaboration systems that utilize project management, closed networks, and e-mail systems, wikis have the benefit of reducing overall e-mail traffic, providing faster, more widespread communication, a common platform that is flexible for multiple uses, and allows for easy access. It also allows for use by anyone involved with minimal training, and adaptability for pretty much anything you may need of them without needing to rescale or change the process of integration. Wikis are generally an easy-to-use, easy-to-maintain platform and can be one of the easiest ways to maintain projects without having to constantly rethink and revise systems in a business.

Implementation Problems

Unfortunately, putting a wiki into place can be a complex process that can hit a few snags, especially in a business environment. While there will be plenty of problems already in existence for any new wiki (as outlined in other parts of this book), these particular problems are known to crop up for businesses in particular:

- Manager Support and Reception from the Environment — Getting management and the general consensus of the office to stand behind a new form of technology, especially when it directly affects how much work they have to do, can be incredibly hard.
- Leader Involvement — Leaders are required to provide interaction with employees, dialogue, and feedback on what is happening within the process. Without leaders to do this, a new wiki can break down quickly.
- Starting at the Right Place — Each office has a different need in terms of where to start building. For some, it is top down and for others it has been bottom up. Effectively recognizing and reacting to the proper method is vital.
- General Consensus on What is Needed — Getting everyone in a team to agree upon and work together toward a goal can be hard. With a collaborative project like a wiki, you not only need teamwork; you need to find adaptability in your peers and creativity to use the new technology.

In many cases, the wiki itself is an incredibly valuable tool no matter how you look at it, but you will need a solid environment in which it can work. Without a business that can effectively flex and change to accommodate a wiki and employees who are willing to attempt the changes, a wiki will often fail to have an impact.

Regardless of the way one looks at the technology though, there is one thing that remains constant across the board. Wikis are built in a way that makes them easy to use and easy to implement. Other knowledge management tools are much harder to implement and require massive volumes of training that do not exist for wiki platforms. If a wiki can be adopted properly, and the business adapts effectively, there are plenty of ways to make a huge leap forward in knowledge sharing and streamlined processes in a business.

Altered Methods of Leadership for New Technology

One of the most vital aspects of growing the use of wikis in an organization is solid leadership. Without a strong leader to control the flow of information and to integrate that flow into the new practices of employees, a wiki will quickly fail due to lack of organized use. A good leader needs to not only lead by example, using the technology, mandating its use, and reminding employees of its presence, they need to follow up when doing so.

A key task here is to remove the barriers that stand in the way of those who may attempt to use a technology. If it takes too long to login into something, the coding is too complex, or the process of moving information from a standard operating channel (such as e-mail or existing project management software) to a wiki is difficult, it will also be scoffed at. Making it faster, easier, and more natural to use a wiki is a vital task for management.

Another way to boost wiki usage as a leader is to push creativity and experimentation in the wiki by showing teams how they can use the wiki for simple tasks and opening it up for them to use the site for more advanced, complicated tasks. Additionally, monitoring the use of the wiki by teams and individuals is a must. If users feel that their use of the wiki is in any way optional, many will choose to stick with what they know instead of adapting to new technology and time-consuming learning processes.

This new method of leadership by using and showing how to use a wiki will not only boost uses of the new platform, but also create an environment where employees and teams are encouraged and excited to jump into it.

Is a Wiki Right for Your Business?

The next question is of course whether a wiki will benefit your business in any particular way. It does no good to spend days and months working to develop a new strategy if it turns out the time spent was all in vain. In most cases, the complete freedom that wikis provide in terms of publishing and sharing information is going to save your company a great deal of time and money and become a very viable option. Enterprise applications were not cheap and still are not very user-friendly for project management, requiring great deals of training. However, wikis are cheap (oftentimes free) and require minimal training or time investment, making them a viable option for office-wide training and implementation.

For this reason, wikis can easily centralize things like business information, spreadsheets, Word files, PowerPoint presentations, PDFs, images, and charts. You can embed information, add e-mails, blog posts, and instant messaging, and combine a great number of wikis for highly interactive, easy to use technology. The biggest drawing point of a wiki is it so largely draws on collaboration. Project management software cannot do this. It is too bulky and focused on specific users (mainly project managers and department heads) where wikis can be used by anyone, updated by anyone, and easily viewed by clients. And while many businesses worry about the open, free to edit nature of wikis, enterprise software almost always has version control, editing access, and page distribution tools included to make it more viable to control who accesses what, and how they use the access they have.

Reasons to Implement a Wiki

The following reasons can be good jumping off points for businesses that may be considering implementation of a wiki:

- Need for a cheap and fast Intranet that has functionality, security, and tangibility for all your needs.
- Publication of a wide array of different documents that need to be available in one simple location without wor-

rying about redundancy and wasted effort.

- Easily manage notes, agendas, calendars, and team related data and plans.
- Project management tool that is cheap, easy, and accessible by anyone in your organization.
- Easily shared documents and a central location for both employees and your clients to view documents.

When to Think Twice

There are going to be certain situations when a wiki may not be ideal for your business. Here are a few examples of when you may want to think twice about this option:

- Complex file format uses. Many wikis support only text or HTML. If you need a more complex wiki, there are some PHP and SQL based platforms out there for bigger file types, but skip PERL based wikis.
- Lack of a leader in your team can cause a wiki to fail quickly. There needs to be someone who can devote time and energy to getting a wiki implemented and your team converted to using it.
- Collaboration may not be a good way for your company to do business. Content management and other more individual and hierarchy-related processes can often be jumbled up when peer review is introduced.
- If you want to have opinions and free sharing of ideas on a wiki, the platform will rarely support such interchange. Blogging may be a better solution for such a need.

Comparing Wikis to Content Management Software

One of the most common questions that a business will ask when a wiki is about to be implemented is why such a simple, cheap software option is any better than CMS, which is widely available and highly regarded. First off, the lack of cost is a major factor. Instead of installing multiple copies of a $100/license piece of software on a dozen computers, companies can now use open source, free options that are much easier to access.

Wikis are also Web based, which makes them much easier to access outside the workplace, increasing off-hours productivity when needed and ensuring the learning curve is slightly less (everyone knows how to use a Web browser). Users will control the wiki in the end as well, which makes administration much easier for those in charge and saves a great deal of time and energy for IT departments.

Wikis are also inherently organized by themselves, meaning you can create and maintain your own ontology and keep it steady throughout the site without having the software trying to tell you how to make it work. Collaboration is also a major part of wikis, making them much easier to operate by a large group of people while boosting creativity many times over. One person working alone is a single mind on a project while a dozen people sharing ideas and building a product is a much more powerful entity.

Who is Using Wikis

There are many different companies out there using wikis right now. Most of the wikis being used in business are in smaller companies with less than a few million in revenue each year, using the new format with fewer employees and more opportunities to try and boost their creativity and productivity and create a new model for future employees.

There are some major companies out there using wikis though. Nokia has long used Socialtext for their development teams while Yahoo!'s employees are big fans of TWiki. Other companies like Kodak, Disney, ATT, Motorola, and GM have begun using wikis freely for different purposes while even the government is now using wiki platform software for things like intelligence sharing. The key to success here is closing the wiki and making it hierarchy based. While the goal of any wiki is collaboration and openness, that can only ever stretch to a certain degree. Without at least a small degree of accountability and access control, even the most efficient wikis can suffer.

Limiting Access to Maintain Quality

In a business, especially when the goal of a wiki is collaboration and building ideas, there is always a problem that can arise where the same individuals use the wiki and others completely ignore it. This can lead to a dearth of ideas, even worse than before a wiki was introduced. Many worry their opinions will not be heard in the cloud of other ideas or they will not receive credit for what they proposed.

To get around this problem, everyone on a team needs to feel that their contributions are both valuable and being heard. To make this possible, the wiki should remain closed, with limited access to only those individuals that should be working on it. By maintaining separate Webs on a wiki that are each closed off to a specific team of individuals who have been assigned to it, you can still support collaboration without causing certain individuals to get carried away and offer too much while others are being ignored.

Ways to Use a Wiki at Work

Simply replacing old systems with something equally as bulky and hard to maintain does not serve anyone. You want to streamline and maximize efficiency, two things that a wiki excels at, but you need to be sure it fits your situation. Before we get started, let us take a look at what a wiki is capable of doing for your business and what that means for you:

Source of Shared Knowledge

The number one thing a wiki can do for you as a business is provide a single database for shared knowledge. Imagine how messy it is to have multiple file cabinets and databases spread throughout various Intranets, closed networks, and desktops that you need to make a phone call, file a requisition form, or go upstairs to access. A wiki makes all freely available knowledge accessible to all members of a business who need to have access to it. It also makes it easy for all members to get into that information and share with others. Because most high-end wiki engines used by businesses offer access control, you can ensure certain Webs within your wiki are access only and do not get changed or rewritten by someone who should not have access to do so.

Cutting Down on Unnecessary E-mails

One thing a wiki does in a business better than many other places is cut down on the e-mail memos that go out to everyone. These e-mails may be ignored, overlooked, or worse yet replied to by a single person when they mean to only talk to the person who sent it. The ambiguity of this form of communication has been known to cause numerous problems and then there is the issue of access to that information. Everyone has the e-mail, but if they all delete it, it may be gone for good.

A wiki offers a concrete database for memos and e-mail information to be sent. A single Web site can be created where all relevant parties are automatically subscribed to the content there. They will receive notifications whenever a new addition is made. Less e-mail, less confusion, and a concrete record of every memo makes for a much easier means of maintaining your communications.

CASE STUDY: MICHAEL DONNELLY

Michael Donnelly works for a Tukwila, Wash., design firm as a project manager where he has maintained and organized projects for much of the last four years. A year ago, he approached his boss about implementing a wiki-based system to make communication between the firm's four different departments easier.

"I have been a project manager for four years now and it is not exactly the easiest thing in the world," Donnelly said. "The design company I work for is constantly changing staff, expanding, retracting, restructuring, etc. The designers do not like to write things down, the writers do not like to map things out, and the bosses do not like to do much of anything. I have to keep it all under control somehow and then maintain some semblance of order with the customer on top of everything else."

"So, I figured I'd start looking for some kind of software that would work better to control things than the project management program that only I knew how to use and only I was able to input updates to," he continued. "I started working with a basic install of MediaWiki to keep my own thoughts in order and soon enough was finding that I could do a whole lot more than I expected with it. I talked to our programmer and he put together a simple closed wiki and then I talked to the boss and he started getting everyone to use it. Like magic, I had somehow cut out about an hour or two a day of running around the office, getting updates on projects, compiling notes and putting them all into my records. People are not only updating their project pages as necessary, they are being much more detailed than they were before when I tried to pester them."

Databases

A solid database of information and content for your work place can make a lot of things much easier to do and access. First of all, you can start making a much more clearly defined attempt to keep information in one place, and second, you can easily access and edit them without having to know the intricate basics of complicated software.

Training

Training is one of the fundamental uses for wikis that has grown the most in many workplaces. There are a few reasons for this. One of the reasons is training materials constantly change. Every week processes and procedures seem to adjust as new things are tried out, old ways are considered obsolete, and the business evolves. This means that a great deal of materials become out of date very quickly, new employees are poorly trained, and your turnover goes up as new entries become confused or lost in their new workplace.

Having a resource in place that provides new employees with up-to-date procedures and a resource they can check back to every now and then for changes makes for an easy, maintenance-free training resource. It allows for self-training more easily, saves on paper, and maintains a single resource that all employees can look to for vital information about their current duties.

Documentation

Having copies of everything is vital especially when you have numerous different departments, hundreds of different people accessing each of those departments, and a slew of different resources coming together at any given time. A wiki provides a depository for documentation across the crux of your business. You can easily access, maintain, research, and call forth old information about any number of different projects, routines, and past actions without having to harass a half dozen coworkers to get the forms they probably have stashed in their desk somewhere.

Spreadsheets

Easily accessible spreadsheets are a common tool in most work-places but how they are operated, accessed, and maintained is a detail that changes constantly. Most workplaces are incapable of a simple and easy to maintain database of spreadsheets that everyone can access for a few reasons. First of all, the technol-ogy behind file sharing software is commonly harder to use than necessary. Second, there are too many different ways they can go wrong. If a file gets checked out on one machine and someone forgets to upload their changes, the file can be inaccessible for hours or days (especially over the weekend). A Web site can be edited in real time and accessed freely by anyone with permis-sion to do so, making shared files much easier to maneuver.

Project Management

Project management is a growing field in which wikis have be-come infinitely more useful. With so many project managers today dealing with a dozen or more clients, numerous depart-ments and personnel members, and a large number of resources overseas, it can be incredibly useful to have a single wiki page for each project that is updated in real time by personnel in each department as they complete tasks. Project managers can auto-mate large chunks of their work and take on more clients this way as well.

A side effect of this change is many project managers are now ca-pable of providing more immediate access to clients to resources regarding their projects. They can show them current progress, detailed breakdowns of how the project is being completed, and allow them to access questions that can be answered directly by the programmers, designers, accountants, project staff, etc.

Putting Together Your Business's Wiki

So, how do you turn all of these potential resources and options into a single plan that your business can use to automate so many different tasks in such a simple, easy fashion? It starts by going through your current systems and comparing them to the re-sources provided by a wiki.

Ask yourself a few simple questions. Can a wiki automate tasks that are currently wasting valuable resources? Can your team benefit from the way a wiki works? Will your team be able and willing to use a wiki and will the resources required to train them be effective?

When these questions are answered you will usually know well if a wiki is going to fit your needs and if you are going to be able to convert your business for effective organization online via a wiki. If you find your current system works well, has few holes in it, and you are generally only going to be expending huge chunks of resources to develop a wiki that you will have to work hard for anyone to use, you may want to rethink your approach to devel-oping a wiki in the first place.

Planning

For any project like a wiki to actually be successful, it needs to be properly planned out in advance. Without planning, the project can devolve into any number of messes very quickly. To start with, treat a new wiki like a project by giving it goals, a timeline, tools, and roles for different people to play in its implementation. It does not need to be a full, monstrous project that absorbs more resources than absolutely necessary, but you should spend time developing a basic plan that works with the wiki to ensure everyone knows their role in its operation.

Collaboration is often poorly managed. It is an inherent flaw that the process has across the board and it has to do with individuals thinking that because users are supposed be working together equally they do not need leadership and they will manage themselves more effectively. This is almost never the case though. Project managers are absolutely necessary and should be included for every project, even a wiki.

The first thing that should be done is all collaborators on a project should agree upon deadlines with all milestones in between carefully mapped out.

Second, someone should be made responsible for packing and delivery of the final product when everyone is finished with their parts of the process. This does not mean putting one person in charge — it means having one person who will make sure nothing is missing and that the project is always on task. This same individual should work to develop a plan for the use of the same software so there are no incompatible files or products. The collaborators should also agree upon what it is they are creating.

By combining a few basic goals, requiring everyone works within the same confines, and going back through all finished products to be sure nothing is missing and no one has forgotten their role, used the wrong file formats, or misplaced anything on the wiki, collaborators can effectively maintain a steady flow of ideas off of each other. In this way a wiki is much more likely to succeed than one where a handful of team members are thrown at a problem and told to figure it out.

[[CHAPTER 5]]

Wikis in the Classroom

A s a teacher, the idea of integrating new technology into the classroom can be both exciting and a bit intimidating. You may understand the technology well, but will your students take to the new opportunities it provides readily? Or, will it be the opposite and find you spending more time learning than your students? The question is a good one, but more and more educators are finding that the technology behind wikis is perfectly fit for helping students learn the more effective and streamlined methods required by so many colleges, careers, and workplaces to succeed. Collaboration is the key to modern commerce. Teaching students early on technologically sound ways to work together can be a huge advantage for them as they develop.

Ten Things to Use a Wiki for in the Classroom

So, what use is a wiki to the classroom? What purposes does this exciting new and strange technological tool provide that students will not only grasp onto quickly, but will be able to learn more effectively with? Here are a few ways that your classroom can directly benefit from a wiki and how to build your lesson plans around it. Remember that a wiki does not have to replace a white board, nor does it need to become the sole resource in your classroom. Like the Internet or a textbook, it is only a single tool among many.

CASE STUDY: VALERIE CARDIGEAN

Like many teachers, Valerie Cardigean was not sure that a wiki would work with her students. Having previously experienced problems with wikis and research in the classroom, her view of them was not only negative, it was exclusionary. However, after reading multiple lesson plans that utilized the platform in unique new ways, she took a chance and was surprised to find that wikis were both agile enough for her rambunctious students, but also an exciting way to build upon existing plans instead of replacing them altogether:

"I was incredibly skeptical of using a wiki at first," Cardigean said. "To be perfectly honest, I was one of those teachers that outright banned the use of Wikipedia in the classroom — and for good reason. You see one paper written directly from Wikipedia, you see a dozen. I had a project last year in which three students plagiarized the same poorly written Wikipedia article — and it was wrong."

"But, the technology itself has been great," she continued. "I could not have asked for a better way to make my students work together. Having a group project was once one of the most feared parts of the semester. Last semester I had multiple comments from students that they would recommend the wiki to other teachers and this semester, there were students excited to use it. There is something relaxing about using a piece of software to share your opinion and information, and even students that would normally slink to the side and remain quiet (unfortunately getting lower grades because of it) are chiming in online, doing the research, talking to each other, sharing with each other. It is incredible — it really, truly is."

Research Projects

In many cases, projects are done in groups throughout many modern classrooms. It makes life a bit easier for a teacher grading classrooms with 30 students and it makes for a good lesson in teamwork and group management in a way that teaches valuable collaborative skills. In the case of a wiki-based research project, providing each group access to a Web site where they will post their resources, contributions, and current progress allows a few different things. First of all, teachers can carefully monitor and watch the students to see how they are progressing. Second, those teachers can more effectively maintain control over the students to be sure they are actively participating in a group, and third, teachers can be sure that the group is not straying from the subject matter on purpose. Instead of asking a group every week or two how they are doing, teachers can now simply look and see where they are, possibly grading them on maintaining their wiki as they go.

Group Grading

Oftentimes, an effective means of grading a group is to have them grade each other. A wiki provides an open way to do this while maintaining the group aesthetic and ensuring that no one feels picked on or underappreciated, either by the group or by the teacher.

Homework Assignments

A common problem that many students have is being able to get access to past homework assignments, reading resources, or other information that they may have missed out on. College professors that do not grade on attendance have been posting lecture notes and syllabi on Web sites for years and a wiki provides a way for every teacher to do just this with minimal knowledge of how to use the Internet, all the while ensuring every student gets what they need. It also negates any claim that a student's dog ate their homework. Now they can just print a new copy.

Literary Projects

Things like group writing projects are always popular in elementary school and English classes and generally require a certain degree of group work. Students will grade each other's work, solicit ideas from each other, and develop their writing style through what they read from their peers. A group resource like a wiki makes it easier to access and maintain these resources.

Reading Lists

Reading lists sent out over breaks, or for book reports, are often coupled up where students need to discuss their selection with the teacher before starting to ensure they do not do the same report as someone else. An online reading list saves the teacher from wasting paper with printouts, and wasting her or his time with having to meet with each student to verify their selection. Have each student mark off which selection they have made, telling the rest of the class which book they will review on a wiki.

Classroom Feedback

Feedback for a teacher is vital in developing a teaching style that allows them to grow as a teacher, teach to the students in that class, and compile a greater way to handle their students in the future. This is especially useful for young teachers who are just learning how to interact with their students. While it requires a certain degree of trust on the part of the teacher, soliciting feedback on a wiki can allow students to be candid and constructive and to learn how to share their ideas on an open forum, something that is becoming more and more common online (and that few people have ever learned how to do politely and constructively).

Summer Assignments

Some schools and teachers require their students to read or produce homework over the summer before they start their class. It can be hard to relay these assignments, especially if at the last minute, the class gets a new teacher. By providing students access to a wiki before the summer, they can read up on the homework assignments, even turning them in before school starts in the fall if they so desire.

Group Discussion

One of the most common problems that students have is the ability to discuss things with each other openly. Teachers have been using technology to tackle this problem for some time. According to Pew Internet Research, nearly 80 percent of all children under the age of 18 are more likely to be open online when they at least feel anonymous (regardless of whether they are or not) than in person with the person they are speaking to. Using a wiki or message board to solicit conversation from a class of students can not only speed up the process but also maintain a progression that students will take with them when they move on to the next grade.

History Lessons

History is a fickle thing. It is written by a select few and the rest of society is left with their differing points of view. While most classrooms are stuck with the lesson plans their schools provide them, a good exercise is to show students how history is developed and how what they learn is only a single perspective of a whole. By having them write their own versions of events into a wiki and compare what everyone wrote and how the final product turned out, the project shows students how a wiki evolves with the writers it has and how history evolves alongside them.

Teaching Manners Online

Online manners are a huge issue for many people. It might not seem like a problem the nation's teachers need to address, but a quick look at the terse language on most forums, blogs, and wikis and the poor quality of many e-mails shows that the future of communications is at a loss for a standardized, well designed method of communication. By teaching students how to be constructive and polite in their posts to a wiki at a young age, students can learn more easily how to communicate in the future.

The Research Dilemma

Many teachers have started to shun wiki technology based solely on the dilemma they are currently facing from sites like Wikipedia. Because the site is so commonly used as a resource site and often is not very useful for anything besides quick research, teachers are growing frustrated with the concept of shared knowledge.

After all, consider how most teachers have grown up and what they were taught in college. Knowledge is not a shared commodity in most academic circles — it is a precious resource that is carefully compiled by the most capable minds and put into a single resource where it can then be disseminated to the masses in a book or a Web site. A wiki turns that idea on its head and creates a culture where knowledge can be easily created and manipulated by nearly anyone with a keyboard. It creates holes in learning and it creates a whole lot of stress and bibliography checking in teachers who get some rather ridiculous sounding essays back from their students.

But, that does not mean Wikipedia or any of the other wiki resources out there are meaningless research sites. First of all, the future of knowledge is going to be shared and collaborative. If we had a collaborative record of history from the last two millennia, most of what we believe to be common knowledge would probably be overturned. After all, those who have the power record history and knowledge. With everyone holding that power today, it is harder than ever before to say anything is "absolutely" correct. Teaching children at a younger age that the world is often a shade of gray, rather than the black and white panache that

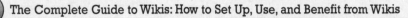
most people see, is a good thing. This is the step forward that many wiki creators longed for when they got started.

Of course, finding the right balance is necessary to be effective as a teacher. Teachers need to know that their students understand key concepts and the basis for those facts, but at the same time, allowing them to gain perspective on knowledge, how it is acquired, and how it is shared should be a fundamental part of the classroom setting as well.

A Sample Study

A good example of how wiki technology has worked its way into the classroom is in Deakin University in Victoria, Australia. Here, about half of all students get their degrees through long-distance or online education. Many subjects may be offered through multiple campuses throughout Victoria or simply off campus and then worked together through online resources. In fact, those students who are working to get a degree in Information Technology must take at least one class online using the online learning environment that Deakin has put into place with their Web site.

Static content is given in basic HTML, PDF, or PowerPoint format while multiple tools are provided for collaboration in the form of message boards, chat rooms, blogs, and wiki software. Additionally, management software for projects and class work are provided for instructors and students who need it.

Surveys of the students found that many were unhappy with online learning because there was minimal interaction and because there was no way to see their assignments, work in a more formal environment, or understand the technology they were using. Most stated that all students did not participate in group discussions (sometimes as few as 30 percent of students would participate).

Because of the lack of interaction and participation, Deakin soon changed its methods and started promoting the use of wikis and putting in place traditional exercises from classrooms to get students started in basic interaction. The first of these exercises was an icebreaker exercise with a list of questions that you need to ask fellow students to fill out. Questions like "find someone who speaks another language" or "find someone with the same car as you" were listed and then placed on the Web site. In a classroom, the exercise would take 20 minutes and involve 20 students and 15 questions.

Online, the same exercise was given two weeks and thread mode in a wiki where they could ask each other the questions. The site was seeded with instructor information to get students started so they could see how it was all supposed to look. Using a basic MediaWiki installation, the class required that students signed their posts using SiT! software so people could see who had posted what and learn about them for their questionnaires. Photos were also encouraged as well.

Guidelines were put into place to show students what they could and could not do (and to counteract concerns over security and vandalism) included keeping things short, simple, and positively written (no negative statements, even self-effacing). Other guidelines included to post often, be nice, and to encourage contribution. It was a simple, nicely written list of rules that were meant to be easy and non-confrontational.

The Results

In the end, 451 students participated in the process, with 68 percent adding content to their user page and 100 percent signing their posts. A total of 87 pictures were uploaded to the site with multiple other pictures uploaded as well to help with answering questions (such as about pets). More than 80 percent of students participated in some way and talked to other students, and many were quite candid and almost all were polite. The platform never crashed and page edits rose sharply the longer the page was active, ending with 2,000 page views daily in the end and 2,000 wiki edits total between the 451 users.

In the end, this process showed that a wiki can be used in a very simple way to introduce a sense of community and closeness to a group that might otherwise feel distant. In a physical classroom, the same rules can be used to great effect to encourage students who might not otherwise participate in class. It allows users to be much more involved with each other, while not feeling alienated or judged as some might in person.

Crafting a Wiki Lesson Plan

There are a number of ways that classrooms are already putting wikis into play for their students. The examples in this book show where the technology is growing and where teachers and students alike are learning new and exciting ways to share that technology with each other. However, being able to implement an effective lesson plan via a wiki is going to require careful attention to all the factors listed above and the lessons learned through the case studies.

Step 1 — Starting at Square One

When teaching any new technology to students, especially those who may not yet be familiar with similar styles of software, you should always start at the beginning. Do not assume anyone can use a Web browser in certain ways or that anyone knows how to use basic word processing editing skills before a certain age. While college students are almost assured to have some basic knowledge of what they are doing, middle school students may not.

To start off, give each student a demonstration of how the wiki works, showing with specific examples what they will be doing with it. Second, make sure to provide a user guide of some sort, either on the wiki or in a printout to show them how to do basic things like upload images, edit text size, or delete something. The basics are vital to get them started and you do not want anyone coming back after the assignment is over and saying they did not know how to do it.

Step 2 — Developing an Implementation Plan

You should develop a plan for how your wiki is going to go up. Do you want to upload it on the first day of class and then have students start to use it slowly, having examples in place before they start any assignments or do you want to upload it on the first day they will use it so they can start fresh? How you will use the wiki will determine how it is installed and implemented, but always make sure to plan ahead. If you decide to do a wiki project and then wait to implement it until the day the project starts, there might be any number of problems that pop up. Have some form of tech support on hand and be ready to handle any questions or concerns that arise from your students right away.

Step 3 — Realistic Expectations

Just because a wiki has been shown to encourage better participation does not mean it always will. If you have a few students that are serial shut-outs, not providing anything to further class discussion, do not expect that they will suddenly open up in a wiki and then grade them against those expectations. Develop a plan that allows all students to be involved without expecting more than is reasonable from them. Then, share your expectations in detail with your students before they start using the wiki. If you can communicate with them exactly what is needed before anything is started, they are much more likely to participate on your terms.

Step 4 — Creating Accountability

Many times, problems with wikis will arise due to a lack of accountability. Students might be allowed to sign up anonymously to the wiki and then post anything they want to encourage use of the wiki. However, if you do not require them to tell you their user name or to sign their edits, this will not matter because there is no way to hold anyone accountable.

The same goes for group projects where a collaborative effort can often breed laziness in a select few students. Each group should have an administrator who not only keeps an eye on participation and contributions, but who also keeps the wiki clean and effective and who reports any potential vandalism or dilemmas between group members.

Step 5 — Voicing the Goal of Your Wiki Up Front

Telling your students you want them to "participate more often" on a wiki is not going to get them any more involved; nor is forgetting to tell them exactly what you expect out of the use of a wiki. Some teachers will install a wiki, set up a class project through it and then neglect to share with the students beyond basic use of the wiki what they are supposed to do.

Be very specific, telling students how often to post at a minimum, what to post, how to post it, what topics to cover, how much to cover, and so on. The more thorough the project description the more likely your students will not become overwhelmed with the new platform and that they will actually participate when it comes time to start contributing to their group's effort.

Step 6 — Monitoring for Results

A very important step is to ensure you take care to record results and provide feedback throughout the project. Without doing this, you are only going to set up students to fail, especially if this is their first time ever using a wiki. It is important to establish the basics of the project early and then check in often to ensure everyone is up to speed. If you develop a four-week project for your students that has them compiling research reports about ancient Babylonian history, check in weekly to ensure they are getting unique content, reputable sources, and full contributions from the entire group.

This is no different than requiring drafts at various intervals for a written paper. You want to be sure that everyone is on the right pace and if they are not you give them the opportunity to fix their mistakes and get to where they need to be.

Step 7 — Building on Past Examples

If you do a wiki project once and something goes wrong, take note of the errors and the problems and build upon it in your next attempt. A wiki is not unlike any other lesson plan. It requires planning and experience together. Plans do not always go off perfectly, and your classes might change year to year as students come and go. You might find that one year your students are not quite capable of using a wiki when they come into the project, but in the next year that more students are familiar with the technology, something that tends to happen as younger students are given access to more technological resources.

Conclusion

Teaching with wikis is a tremendous way to develop teamwork, collaboration, and creativity in your students and to mix up your lesson plans in a way that will engage young people of all ages. Because wikis are so flexible and so easy to set up, the possibilities for what you do are endless and as more and more classrooms start using technology like this to keep track of work, more options are opening up. It is only a matter of time until wikis, like e-mail before them, become commonplace in every classroom.

[[CHAPTER 6]]

Using a Hosted Wiki Service

It is hard to give a clear walkthrough of a hosted wiki because there are so many out there with so many different options. However, because it is so popular and used so often for things like K - 12 classes or developing a low scale wiki, we will look at **Wikispaces.com** as our example.

Getting Started

When you first visit Wikispaces.com, you will find that the Web site is built and developed in a way that is easy to start for nearly anyone. With thousands of K - 12 teachers, and small groups using the site for their wikis, it is no wonder that there are so many tools and methods implemented to make it a bit easier for the casual user to get started with a wiki.

After you first visit Wikispaces.com, create your account, making sure to pick a solid user name, e-mail address that you do not mind having attached to the account, and a password that is well built so that it cannot be cracked and used to access your account. Now, press join and you should be ready to get started.

Signing Up

On the front page of Wikispaces, you will see a simple "Get Start-ed" box. It will ask you for your user name, password, and e-mail address. Make sure to give an e-mail address that you use for things like this, not a work related e-mail address. Also make sure to pick a good password that no one could guess or use on their own to access your page and make changes or play around with things and cause problems.

After you have done this, Wikispaces will send you an e-mail that tells you to confirm that you signed up for their site. Simply click on the link in your e-mail inbox and you will be returned to the Wikispaces page to start filling in the basics of your account.

To get started, click on the "Make a New Wiki" link and you will be taken to the basic interface to start putting together your first wiki.

What Kind of Wiki?

Choosing what kind of wiki and the name for that wiki is up next. You need to choose whether you want a public, private, or protected wiki. The public wiki is the free version while the pri-vate wiki will cost $5 a month after the initial 30 days and allows you to maintain invitations for the users who have access. The protected wiki is also free and can be viewed by anyone but only edited by those you invite to work on the wiki.

The best way to practice and get started is to start with a pro-tected wiki to maintain control over who can access it. Later, you can change it to a public wiki or a private wiki if you decide you want to open it up or close it down to further viewers or users.

The name of your wiki is an equally important part of this decision. You should pick something that is eye-catching and directly related to the topic of your page. For instance, if you are writing a wiki about rock climbing locations, calling your wiki "John's Place" is not going to help anyone who is actually looking for a wiki about rock climbing locations. So, make sure to pick something that will actually call out for your target audience.

If you are starting a wiki that is related directly to a classroom or workplace, you will want to ensure you pick something related to your work or classroom, but not specific enough to elicit other people to enter and try and sign up for your page. For example, your classroom wiki name may be "Mrs. Johnson's Wiki." It is not specific to anyone but the students in your classroom that way.

Finally, make the decision as to what type of wiki you would like to create. There is a drop down menu here and it is completely optional as all wikis are pretty much the same, but it helps Wikispaces learn more about its demographics and who is using the site. Your options are: "K - 12, Higher Education, Business, Personal, Non-Profit, Government, or Other." Yours should fit nicely into one of those categories.

For our wiki, we are going to go ahead with our rock climbing wiki and choose a name that helps our audience find what we are writing about — in this case "rockclimbingplaces.wikispaces.com." This address will allow our users to quickly and easily find information about rock climbing when they type it into the search engine

Now you can get started making pages and figure out what you want to write about. This part is entirely up to you — we are not going to go through your topic choice — but you can start working on the pages with a short tutorial here on creating pages.

Your Blank Wiki

When you have created your wiki, Wikispaces will take you to your default editing page for that wiki. There are going to be quite a few options on the screen, so let us take a closer look at a few of them so you can see what is involved in working on and maintaining your wiki.

The Top Bar

At the top of the screen you will find the name of your wiki along with a small logo for Wikispaces (a bonsai tree). Next to that you will find the name of the current page, which should currently be "Home" when you have first started your wiki and have not yet added any new pages. Atop the page is your account name, an arrow that allows you to search for other wikis and access other wikis you have created, a mail icon for any e-mails you have received from users on Wikispaces or from visitors who want to talk to you, a button for "My Account" that will take you back to your default account page, a help link for basic information about the site that you may need, and finally a button to log out of the site.

This is all the basic information that will help you navigate your account and will only appear when you are logged in as the administrator of the wiki.

The Edit Bar

The Edit Bar is a standard bar that shows up at the top of any wiki type or engine out there and will be something you get very familiar with as you edit or own your own wiki. Here is a breakdown of what each page will allow you to do:

Edit This Page

This button will take you to the default editing input for this page. Wikispaces has a WYSIWYG editing input that allows you to edit content and input it like you would in a word processor. However, if you are working with a built in wiki engine like WikiMedia, you may need to use wiki code directly to enter the information it requests here. It is always best to assume you need to know both parts of the page before you start doing anything. Wikispaces will also give you a text editor option, located at the top of the page, which will allow you to edit the page in traditional wiki markup text mode.

Page

The page tab will take you to the current page view if you are looking at any other page at a given point in time. When you click on this button, you will also get a number of additional tool options that allow you to see multiple details about the page. The first option is "Print," which will create a print-friendly version of the page without the sidebars and links. You can also see a "What Links Here?" page that is standard to all wiki pages, showing you which wiki pages link to the one you are currently viewing. "Rename" and "Delete" are administrator tools that can be used to change the basic format of any given page, allowing general access to the content.

"Redirect" will allow you to change where the page points to, and is a valuable tool if you change the name of the page at any given point in time and "Lock" will allow you, as the wiki owner, to keep anyone from editing the page. This is an important tool for teachers and business owners alike who need to maintain some small bit of control over the content on their wikis.

Discussion

The discussion page is a vital aspect of any wiki page and is where users go to talk about changes they want to make and ways to go about making those changes. For your wiki, you need to be sure to maintain a small bit of control over what is posted here by not allowing people to get into heated debates over controversial issues, but also ensure that you allow a healthy debate as it will draw more users and interest to your wiki.

History

The history page is a vital tool that allows you to see what was changed, when it was changed, and the various different versions of a page between changes. If vandalism occurs, this is the link that you will use to get into the back pages of your wiki and rollback those changes. You can also see who specifically changed what in this view.

Notify Me

This link will allow you to create notifications for yourself whenever content is changed. It will send an e-mail to you right away when a new change occurs and tell you what happened so you can more easily monitor vandalism.

The Left Side Bar

The left side bar in a wiki is going to be different depending on the wiki you are using and the options you select. Let us take a look at a few of the options here in a Wikispaces wiki so you can see exactly what you will be dealing with in at least one resource.

New Page

The new page link will allow you to create a new page directly without having to make links first. It is recommended, however, that you do not do this unless you are creating basic starting pages from which to link. A wiki's strength lies in its navigation, meaning you need to create and have links between pages as often as possible. If you fail to create these links and maintain them, the wiki may be a bit harder to get around and some pages may never show up.

Recent Changes

This is an extension of the history page and will show you all the changes that were made in recent calendar days to the wiki. This will allow you to catch up on changes if you are away for a few days or to see how many people are currently participating on your wiki to start with.

Manage Wiki

This button will take you to a slew of administrative tools that your wiki engine provides. Most hosted wikis will provide a great deal of options while wiki engines you install are limited by what you install and activate. Let us take a look at what Wikispaces provides here:

- About — This section will contain details about the wiki including when it was created, by whom it was created, the members of the wiki, your current license, and your current subscription plan. You can directly edit and change the current license to reflect your desires here. By default it will be set to the Creative commons attribution share-alike 3.0 license that basically means anyone can use it for anything if it is not commercial. If you decide you want to alter that license, click on the link and you will be taken to a listing of other licensing options.

- Content — This will allow you to sort through the content in your wiki by pages, files, templates, tags, or via a content manager. It is basically a way to see everything that has been created or uploaded to your wiki in a more visual space.

- People — People will allow you to access and edit permissions and content for the members of your wiki. You can see who is signed up, what permissions they have been given, and invite new members to join. For a content or community wiki, this might not be as important as for a classroom or business wiki where content control is vital to maintaining order on your wiki.

- Settings — There are settings here to change the look and feel of your wiki, the current subscription plan (you can upgrade to paid memberships for more features), add a domain name you have purchased to your wiki, change the basic wiki information that appears for your wiki, or delete the wiki outright.

- Tools — A slew of tools are also included here that allow you to manage your notifications, see the statistics for your wiki including recent views, edits, changes, members, etc. You can also see how much space has been used on your account, review the badges that have been received or given for assistance by your members, check the Web folders for your wiki content, directly import a blog post via an RSS feed, or export the contents of your wiki in an HTML or Wikitext file for backups. This is a very important feature that will allow you to keep detailed records of your wiki from certain days (as the history will only go back so far).

Search

The search box is located directly below the manage wiki link and will allow you to search your wiki for content. This can be altered in your options as well to affect how it operates.

Navigation

The last section on the left side bar is the navigation section. You will be able to edit the navigation section to display whatever links, categories, or subcategories you want. This is a good way to create root pages for access by your members and visitors without having to interlink unrelated pages. Always make sure to establish a good linking and navigation plan before you start making pages. See the chapter on Ontology and Navigation for more information on how to do this.

The Page Content

When you create your first page, it is going to be blank with a link at the top that says "This page does not exist yet. You can create it by clicking the Edit Button." This will appear on every page you create that does not yet have content. This includes pages you link to that do not yet exist (the recommended method to use for making new pages).

Along with this link atop the page, the page will include some basic information to help you get started. These sections will all disappear as soon as you create the first page and start adding content to your wiki.

Getting Started

Getting started will tell you where to start with the edit button as well as some information about commenting and discussions.

About Your Wiki

This section will give you links to edit basic things from the manage wiki page including settings, look and feel, permissions, and members.

Need Help?

This will point you to the help section for more information about how to use Wikispaces and wikis in general.

Contact Us

You will be given a link directly to help@wikispaces.com here so that if you have any questions right away, you can ask them.

Creating Your Wikispaces Pages

To get started, there are two ways to make a new page in a wiki. You can either use the "New Page" tool or you can create a link to a new page from an existing page and then click on that link to go to the editing page to create a new one. The second method was used for original wikis to ensure all pages were linked to at least one page. That standard is still maintained today on many wikis, requiring links for pages.

For this reason, you should almost never use the "New Page" button if you can avoid it. First of all, it creates problems when you try to go back and create navigation after the fact. If you start with a root page and create links from there for all subsequent pages, it is easier to find your pages. Wikipedia, for example, requires that all pages created have at least two links to them from established pages elsewhere. It is important for this reason to do the same for any wiki you create. It establishes legitimacy and it enforces that your members do not go through and start adding random content as they see fit whenever they want to create a new page.

What a Page Needs

Another important factor to consider for any new page on a wiki is what content it needs to include to be considered valuable enough to be a new page. There are many different standards that wikis will use to decide what should be included in a new wiki page. Some wikis require that a wiki page have at least a certain number of different sections included for each page before it can be uploaded. Others require that you have at least three different citations from outside sources.

You need to establish what your baseline for a new entry is as well so your members can know immediately what they are allowed to enter into a new page. For a content wiki, this is much more important than a process wiki where the rules will probably be laid out regardless of the format.

Content Wiki Requirements

Content wikis are based upon having unbiased, reliable information, otherwise you are going to have trouble finding people willing to read your wiki. Most content wikis will use the following basic rules for new content:

Links

You need to link from a certain number of pages to the new page (usually two). This ensures other content is related to the new content and that you are not randomly listing information on your wiki.

Citation

There needs to be reliable outside sources to quote for this information. This can include links to articles, blog posts, forums, or official Web sites. Usually, having more than one citation is required. This will vary depending on the style of wiki you are building.

Content

The content of your wiki needs to be uniform and well structured. For this reason, each page should represent the overall content guidelines of the wiki. New pages should be built into the navigation of the wiki, not added on to it. This means you should try to avoid duplicate information as well. Do not allow new pages for content that could fit into an existing page.

Process Wiki Requirements

Process wikis are different because they usually come from the top down and will include a number of pages that are requisite. In most cases, members will not add new pages to the wiki because that is not what they are there to do. Have an administrator (or yourself) build the wiki structure up so each page serves a purpose. If you are planning a wedding, you probably do not need bio pages for the bride's cousin Joe. You do however need a page for current menus. The same can be said for classroom wikis where a teacher needs to clearly define the role and purpose of each page in a wiki so the students know where to put their new content, how to interact with the pages, and what (if any) new pages they are allowed to create.

Community Wikis

The community wiki operates in much the same way as a process wiki in this regard. More than likely you will probably not need anyone to create new pages, but if you do, you should probably make sure you do it in a way that allows anyone to create a page in the same fashion. For example, if our Rock Climbing wiki members decide they want to start creating pages for outings without the oversight of the administrator, they should know where to put those new pages, how to format them, and what to link them to. Create a structure to do this and you will make maintenance of those pages much easier to handle. The same is true for nearly any kind of club, grouping, or community-oriented wiki project. Make sure to maintain standards, tell your users where and how to add content, and monitor the content they add as they add it.

Security and Protection

One of the things about Wikispaces that has made it so popular with teachers and small businesses is the ability it provides to easily and quickly protect your content. You can choose to allow anyone to edit the wiki, or you can choose to block access to a select few individuals who know the content and the purpose of the content they are creating. To effectively manage your security on Wikispaces, you will use the Manage Space option in the Settings area. When you do so you can change the type of wiki you are operating to one of the following:

- Public — This will make your wiki viewable to anyone that comes across it and subsequently make it possible for anyone to edit.
- Protected — This will make it so anyone can view the pages that you put into your wiki but so that only a select few members that you have approved may actually edit the page you have created.
- Private — This makes it so pages can only be viewed or edited by members you have given access to. You need to pay the Wikispaces premium to actually use this feature though; however, the cost is relatively minimal.

From here, you can simply allow sign-ups to the wiki or create user names to access the wiki in any way you like. It makes it easy to control the access of your wiki and to ensure outside influences do not interrupt or interfere with what you are trying to create.

The Premium Membership

Wikispaces is much like any other hosted wiki service and provides an option for a paid service plan that will allow you access to additional features for a small fee. In the case of Wikispaces, that small fee is $5 a month or $50 a year and includes the following features:

- No advertising on your pages — The ads that appear on your wiki will be removed.
- Complete Privacy — You can make your wiki 100 percent private by blocking it from viewers or editors. This is a must-have feature for businesses or non-profits.
- Create Custom Themes and Style Sheets — This allows you to create themes with the Wikispaces tools to streamline the interface of creating a new page.

Other wikis will also charge you by bandwidth or space used, making the size of your wiki and how many members you have a factor in the pricing plan that you are given as well. Another cool feature that Wikispaces provides is Private Label creation of wikis in which you can purchase an entire space of wikis to create multiple sites. Schools, purchasing a wide swath of wiki space and then doling it out to teachers and clubs to use as needed, often use this. This is also a paid upgrade feature and can be found in that screen.

Conclusion

Wikis are going to vary between every Web site you use and every hosting service you encounter, but for the most part everything in this chapter is static enough that you can take the lessons learned here and apply them to just about everything. This does not mean that you will find the exact same setup or that your wiki will have as many options as Wikispaces. In many cases, wikis have far fewer options and opt for simplicity and ease of use rather than full access. But, by being prepared for the basic aspects — the document, editing, thread, and history modes as well as the tools that are behind the scenes helping you make your wiki better — you will find a slew of free and paid options out there to help you get your wiki off the ground.

[[CHAPTER 7]]

Wiki Structure and Ontology

The structure and ontology of a wiki is one of those things that are incredibly vital to being successful with your wiki. The basis of the wiki may be free collaboration, but if it was not organized well, no one would want to use his or her wiki for anything more than a fun side project. What makes Wikipedia so effective is that every category is well created and cross-checked with links between pages and a very functional search mode that helps you get to where you need to be.

You need to decide early on, well before you start adding pages, how you will create the ontology of your wiki and what your navigation structure will be. The visual aspects, themes, colors, and skins are all equally as important and without a clear visual idea of what you are building before starting, you might be faced with quite the mess. In this chapter we are going to cover not only the basic structure of the wiki you are creating but the linking of those pages to each other, linking outside your wiki, and using things like tags and uploading external files to your wiki to add a bit of extra oomph to your content.

Structuring a Wiki Effectively

A wiki can be compared to any number of things. People like to think of them like spider webs or as a smaller analogy to the Internet. Others like to compare them to dictionaries or encyclopedias, if only because of the obvious similarities that sites like Wikipedia have created in the two. But, wikis are really a structure unto themselves. They need and require that you, as their creator, know exactly how the site should look before content starts being added. This is important because at some point you relinquish a lot of the control over how the site grows and develops. If you did not put into place a good ontology and structure, you are going to have one heck of a mess on your hands by the time your incoming new members are through with the site.

Ontology and Structure

The information on your wiki needs to be put into categories, and those categories need to not only be effective — they need to be the exact fit for the information. You do not want to have a slew of extra, superfluous categories that do not make a whole lot of sense. For that reason, it is vital that you sit down and figure out how many different categories, page types, and directions your wiki is going to strike out in. Even a site like Wikipedia has its limits, disallowing or at least calling into question pages that are too similar to other pages or content that appears in multiple locations instead of one central page.

So, to keep everything nice and neat, we are going to break it down in the same way a biologist might categorize the species of birds. Starting from the top with their kingdom (Animalia), birds are broken down by kingdom, phylum, class, order, family, genus, and species. A wiki has the same basic structure, with the wiki itself being the entire category for everything you put on your domain, a Web of content being a smaller, self-contained category of content, and a page within that site containing a very specific amount of information about the topic.

The hard part is not understanding this but putting it into practice and creating smaller subsets on your wiki that effectively break down and organize the content on it without creating too much to navigate or doubling over on any topics. Your classroom, for example, might create different Webs for each homework assignment or for each week of the semester. The content that goes into the Web will often decide how it gets broken down in the long run. To give you an idea of what you are looking at in your own structure, here are a few common ways that people break down the content on their wikis and how their methods can help you do the same for yours:

- Natural Groupings — Certain things just have natural groupings and can make your life a little easier if you simply follow those groupings. For example, you can quickly and easily put together a wiki about films and group them by director or genre. You can describe books by their authors and can describe music by album or by artist. These groupings are naturally included but whatever method you decide on should be standardized throughout the wiki for the sake of navigation.
- Charts — Oftentimes businesses have need of detailed, well-organized charts of information. If you want to utilize a chart for your information, you should maintain a few key details, breaking down that information from the top

of the chart to the bottom. Do not just randomly plug information into pages and say it all came from the same chart.

- Actions — Project management relies on actions in a project and they can easily be grouped together in that way. If you have a design firm where certain tasks are carried out by certain people — concept, computer visual, copywriting, print, and cropping, etc. — you can categorize tasks that need to be accomplished by their location in the hierarchy of tasks that each person needs to accomplish that week, month, or year.

- Alphabetical — The simplest of all taxonomies is by alphabetical order and can make your job a lot easier if the content has no other discernible pattern. Before using this pattern make sure to consider how your visitors will expect to find the content. If there is a more reasonable way, use it.

- Space and Time — There might be specific tasks that need to be completed in a set time, such as Monday, Tuesday, or Wednesday, or by specific branches of a business. If your wiki revolves around such delineations, breaking down the content in such a format can be a highly effective way of presenting it more easily.

- Location — Breaking down a wiki geographically can be done easily as well if it makes sense. Travel wikis, content wikis about certain places, or project related wikis with international clients (and time zones) might benefit from this type of structure.

These are just a few examples of different ways that you might consider breaking down your wiki. If you can think of others, do not hesitate to use them as they may be the best way to organize, access, and maintain your content.

Patterned Linking

This is a very important aspect of how you build your wiki because it directly has to do with how the people who view your wiki will interact with the information. It is too hard for many people to consider how something is going to delineate from a long string of different categories, which is why you generally try to maintain a few set categories with smaller pages in them. If you do not do this properly, you are only going to waste everyone's time trying to track down the page. If you create content that naturally groups together, you can more easily combine the information onto different pages. For example, you might have a pair of pages that describe different versions of the same thing but that both link to the same project goals. It works because the linking structure is set up to work.

Easy Linking

Think about the way links work on wikis for a second. Pages quickly and easily connect to each other because they use a simple linking structure with a "[[link]]" tag. As you can imagine, the ease of actually integrating and using those links so none of them are broken is going to be highly important in making sure the pages your users create are not pointing to a dozen different possible pages that do not exist. You should thus create a standardized format for naming your pages that anyone can remember after a few uses.

For example, if you are creating a wiki that uses geography as its common theme — maybe you are doing a travel wiki for Eastern Asia — you should decide how page names will be created. You might decide that all place names will be created as just the city name. This will allow anyone that creates a link in a page to know that they need only link the city name. You may create pages in a structure like "CountryCityname" so they know to latch them together for ease of breaking down the content.

In most cases, linking like this is unnecessary for content-driven wikis but is highly valuable when you start breaking down process wikis. Say you create multiple projects for the same company and link all the proposals for those projects on the same wiki and you need to delineate between each one. An easy way to do this is to use a structure like "ProposalCompanynameDate." Every page that is a proposal would start with "Proposal," followed by the company it is written for and its date. It would not only make finding the proposals much easier (you now know the date and company in each title), but it also makes linking to them easier as well because there is a standardized format for each one.

And, if you use a complicated linking format that you would rather not show in each page, you can hide the real name of the link by using the following tag:

[[ProposalCompanynameDate] [Proposal]]. This tells it to display only the word "Proposal" for the link instead of all that other text. Make sure you do not create a Web that says simply "Proposal." This could refer to any number of different categories on your wiki and can cause great confusion if you are not careful.

Creating the Navigation Structure

Once you have decided on the format you are going to use to break down the content on your wiki, you need to start structuring the paths through your wiki to that information. This will allow you to decide which links you will place on your front page, on your support pages (with category and section links), and your content pages.

Your Front Page

The front page is a vital tool in your wiki, showcasing the content when your visitors first arrive at your wiki and giving them a means by which to navigate through your content with ease. You are going to need to create a direct method to get from one point to another via your front page, linking to vital points in your wiki without over doing it (you do not want a huge list of links to confuse everyone that comes to your wiki).

Who is Your Audience?

The type of content you place on your front page will be affected slightly by who happens to be interested in the content. If your wiki is a content wiki, you are going to want to advertise you are looking for content to be added, give links to the most valuable content available, and then provide a walkthrough of how or where to add content. People want direction and this is where you will give it to them.

If you are writing for a process wiki, you should instead focus on organization and access. If it is for project management, create a complete list of all the projects in your wiki up front so they can be easily accessed and worked with by your visitors. If it is for a task, show the steps in the task clearly for easy access and use.

For a community wiki, you should focus on showcasing the various interests and fields of study for your community. For example, if you create a rock climbing wiki that showcases where to find the best conditions around the country, you should show some information about rock climbing grading, the current conditions in a few key places, and a select topic that you think your audience would like to know about right now.

Other things to consider in how your front page looks are what the people arriving already know about your wiki. If it is a content wiki that is advertising via search rankings, the people may not know that it exists or why they should be interested in it to start with. In this case, they will need a boost from someone to tell them what they are seeing and why they should care. If your visitors know that they should be adding content, forget telling them what they are seeing and tell them how to use the wiki. Immediately link to instructions and templates for their use. Finally, if you know that your users are well versed in wiki use, you can tone down on too many instructions, but if they are newcomers to this type of technology, you can never have enough in the way of directions and documentation to help them use the wiki.

Your Section Pages

The next sets of pages you will design are the pages on which you create links to various sections and categories. These are vital for people who are going to browse for content. While many people rely on search, they may not be able to on your wiki, especially if it is lacking in content. Having a good section page will allow them to see what does and does not exist on your wiki and then to plug it into the right location instead of randomly at the end of the wiki where no one will ever find it. Sections should be clearly defined, easily navigated, and quick to adopt as users navigate your Web site.

The Navigation Tools

Every wiki has a series of navigation tools that will appear on every page and that you should utilize with care. This includes the sidebar, the header, and the footer of the page. If you properly implement these features into your wiki, you can greatly help your users navigate through your content and reach what they are looking for without having to stumble around finding the section page again.

For the most part, the header and footer will provide the architecture of the page currently being viewed, including its parent categories or sections and the path back to the main page that the page takes. The sidebar can do any number of things including a more detailed version of the top and bottom bars or offering related pages, search options, login info, or simply a few stats about the page being viewed. Most wikis will automatically generate all of this content for you so you can usually ignore it, but if you notice that it is not appearing effectively, you should make a few vital changes to how the different content looks to be more functional for your audience. Here are some tips to doing just that:

Your Headers

There are a few select things that almost all headers do and that you should make sure are in your wiki's header:

- Breadcrumbs — Breadcrumbs are a vital tool for anyone that is using a wiki to gather information. It allows them to see where they have come from on different pages and how to get back to the original category or page they visited. This might say "You Are Here" or "Path."

- Tags — This will show which categories or tags are related to the page currently being viewed.

- Search Box — The search box is almost always in the top right corner and allows for quick and easy access to the search function on the page.

- Jump Boxes — These are the tabs at the top right or in the middle of most wikis that will immediately take users to the pages for editing, attaching, printing, or logging in. These are vital on a wiki as they allow users to interact with the content and make their changes as they see fit.

Generally speaking, if you feel like there are enough tools so your users can find anything they need in the wiki, then you have created an effective header.

Your Footers

The footer will contain a few basic things that can make it easier to navigate your wiki as a whole from any given content page on the network. Most of the time the links will be the same as in the header, except broken down into more specific categories. The same edit, attach, and print buttons will be there along with ways to view backlinks, a history, and additional actions that can be taken from this page.

Sidebar

The sidebar can be used for any number of things and most wiki platforms will give you open access to make changes to this with ease so you can showcase whatever your readers want to see in it right away. Here are some examples of what you might see in the sidebar:

- Support Pages — Links to various support pages on the wiki including documentation of the software, current editorial guidelines, or just plain help files for use on the pages.
- FAQs — Frequently asked questions as well as a forum to ask those questions for users of the site. With a user-operated Web site like a wiki it is vital to have a means by which your users can share their questions and get them answered relatively quickly.
- Search — A search box or forum where users can access and direct content with the click of a button. This is very simple and present in all wikis.
- Recent Changes — A list of recent changes to the wiki as a whole or to the page the user is currently viewing.
- Newsletters or Notifications — A way for users to sign up and get e-mails whenever a change is made to the wiki, the wiki itself is altered, or you want to invite them back. These are highly useful for community wikis. Notifications can also be set on specific pages so users get e-mails whenever a change is made to the content on a given page. This is incredibly useful for process wikis so project managers or office managers do not need to sit by and wait for the changes to appear. They will be notified automatically, even if the employee forgets to send an e-mail.
- Subscriptions — You can subscribe to an RSS feed of the wiki itself or of various pages so you can view all new pages, updates, and changes as they are made in real time. Almost all wiki engines have RSS support.

Visual Changes to Your Wiki

Wikis can have a great number of different things added to them to give them a visual bump — adding a bit of color, some images, or just a different vibe than the typical, standard MediaWiki style interface. You do not need to use color just to spice up your pages either. Color is used in many different ways to add functionality to a wiki and to make it easier to navigate. For example, you might color different parts of a page to indicate different sections and to make it easier to see what you are looking at. Many wikis will color tables for quick color coding. Were one to look at the list of senators from Illinois, the democrats are listed in blue and the republicans in red. Our brains pick this up almost immediately and make that connection, adding valuable information to the page with a simple color tag.

There are a variety of ways to change how your wiki looks and most wikis will provide a slew of tools to make it even easier. In the long run though, you are going to find that the best way to do this is to ensure your changes are actually functionally necessary. Graphic design can be tricky in this way if you are not careful. You can quickly and easily start breaking down the content if you do not stop to think what your changes will actually affect when you make them.

Themes and Skins

The easiest and most accessible way to change the look of your pages is to use a theme or skin that is provided by your software. If you are hosting your own wiki, this will often require some installation. If you are using a hosted wiki, you will almost always have access to a listing of different themes and skins that can easily and quickly be integrated into the content. Each theme will usually have a set font, images, and graphical interface already integrated into each page. You click on the theme to install or activate it and it sets itself up for quick and easy use.

Personalization, Stylizing, and General Rules for Images in Your Wiki

There are a number of different ways in which your wiki might utilize colors and images, but you should be sure that there is a good reason first. Simple black text on white space is basic but it works. People respond to it and no one thinks ill of it, if only because it is so standardized. If you want to be effective in adding color and images, make sure you are adding value to the page. This includes coloring in table entries, adding different colors to sections on the page, and adding images that will personalize your content. For example, you might add a logo for your company or your community group in the upper right or left hand corner. This immediately makes it easier to recognize the purpose of the wiki while branding it as related to your purpose. It looks good, is simple, and has a purpose.

Always keep this in mind when adding colors or images to your wiki to ensure they are useful and not just ways to spice it up for no reason.

Template Use on a Wiki

While you do not want to start telling people how they should create their content, a template can be a very useful tool in showing to them what you would prefer and what other people have done before them. You do not want every page on a wiki to look completely different because someone else put it together, and you do not want to start having to clean up content that is too messy because someone got a little lazy with the editor. Having templates can go a long way in repairing this problem by ensuring you not only develop an effective and standardized means of presenting your information, but that your users follow those standards.

Hosted wikis will showcase a number of templates that you can use from day one and that allow you to easily tell your users how the pages should look. They will have the option to use templates when they create new content and you can dictate which ones to consider. The templates will generally create a page and then present a slew of open-ended content that you can then go into and add or delete things from.

This has a few different values. First of all, it ensures all the different parts of a page you want included are included. Things like dates, times, costs, and specific meetings will be included in the template of a project proposal and will thus need to be filled in by the person who uses that template. They also make your wiki easier to navigate as different users will always find the same content when they visit the page and see the basic format they are used to.

Consider implementing templates in every page you create for simple and easy access to information. Content wikis are a bit less rigid in that most content can be displayed in different formats and still effectively represent itself. However, if you have a section of your wiki about Japanese film that includes the films of certain directors, you may consider using a template so all of those pages are similarly designed and displayed when completed.

Conclusion

By setting up your wiki to effectively utilize the built-in tools that create top notch ontology's and navigation throughout the Internet, you can do quite a few things. You can make an easier to use wiki, a better looking wiki, and ultimately a wiki that gets more visits through search engines and outside linking. When used ineffectively, a giant mess can occur, creating the same problem that has brought down thousands of oversized Web sites. Remember to maintain a steady pace in growth, a keen eye for any problems that might signify a breakdown in structure, and always look for ways to make your wiki faster and better looking.

[[CHAPTER 8]]

Linking and Categorizing Your Wiki

When you start linking and categorizing your wiki, you need to establish a basic format that can be followed throughout the wiki. In the case of wikis like Wikipedia, this is done easily by making sure that the links are all prepared in the same format and that content is always maintained in an easily recognizable database of categories.

Linking between pages does a number of things for your wiki. It not only makes it easier for users to find the content they are looking for; it makes it easier for them to see what needs to be edited. It also makes it much easier for search engines to find your wiki as they tend to like all those internal links pointing back and forth to your content.

Linking Pages on a Wiki

The links on a wiki are entirely different than the links you might find on a Web site. For that reason, many people make fundamental mistakes in how they approach them and edit them when they start using a wiki and editing it constantly. Wiki links are not only more powerful and more useful than Web site links, but they are much easier to create and access and generally much easier to maintain. They do not require complicated code and they do not require that a page even exists when you link to it. They just require a few short keystrokes and the desire or intention to create a new page in the wiki.

Page Names

Unlike Web sites as well, each page on a wiki needs a completely unique name for you to link to it. This is because you are not linking to a Web site address that is already unique; you are linking to a database entry that is only described by the page name you gave it. If you name two pages "Proposals" you will not be able to link to either of them independently, and your wiki may not even be able to delineate between the two. Luckily, most wikis will not let you create two pages with the same name because of how they are structured. It can save a lot of time and confusion in your new users and ultimately works well for linking this way.

Another thing that unique naming can do is that you can easily have multiple Webs with different names for the content so that each have their own structured sub-pages without having to worry about confusion when users search or look for them in the section pages. For example, if you create a wiki about rock climbing locations and then enter a dozen different mountains into your wiki to start, they each have their own Web and unique names, so you can then create pages for each of them that include "Grades," "Current Conditions," or any other information that might justify a stand-alone page.

Two Types of Linking

There are two types of linking used in wikis that still work today, one of which was created by Ward Cunningham back when the wiki format was first developed. The first of these two methods is Camel Case linking and it is the most simple of the two. However, it is also much less versatile in terms of what can actually be done with the format. The second format is Free Linking and is what we have already discussed in this book, showing you how to develop links using brackets that allow for case sensitivity, spacing, and alternate naming. Here is a breakdown of how each type of linking works:

Camel Case

Cunningham first developed Camel Case linking as a method of linking that would work on the fly within a wiki without needing any special markup. The basic premise is you can write the name of the page out with capital letters to delineate the start of each word in the chain and then the wiki will automatically link to it. Here is an example:

- Your page is named Widow's Peak Conditions.
- To link to this page, you would use WidowsPeakConditions.

The Camel Case link has humps in the middle where capital letters appear (like a camel) and the wiki platform knows to automatically link this word to the page by the same name. Each string needs to start with a capital letter, cannot have any spaces, and needs to have at least two upper case letters in a row with at least two lower case letters separating them.

Today, a large number of wiki engines will not use Camel Case linking and will turn it off because it is not a viable means of linking your pages together. It does not have the freedom and uses that Free Linking has. However, if the format works for your needs and you like it, you can almost always turn it on via the options for your wiki.

Free Linking

The second kind of linking and the one that most wikis trend toward (and that Wikipedia uses) is called Free Linking. Ironically, free linking is a bit more precise in how it works, requiring specific tags to call the link, but it is also much more versatile in that you can access and maintain many more kinds of links with the tags that you use.

Free Linking is the basic format we have discussed already that uses brackets such as this: [[Widows Peak Conditions]]

This links the page to the exact case match of the text entered into the brackets and makes it easier to showcase the exact text as you would like it to appear on your page (without having to mess with your spacing). If you create a link with free linking to a page that does not yet exist, you will create that page automatically when you save your page with the link in it. Links to pages that do not yet exist will be red in the text and when clicked on will show you the page that needs to be created along with options to create the page.

There are a few things you can do to take advantage of this as well and create different formats for your links. If you have text you would like to add to the end of the link, you can simply attach it to the brackets, such as making a link plural without having to create a second page for that link. You can also use different text in the link without having to create a new page:

[[Widows Peak Conditions] [Current Conditions]]

Another way to do this is to use: [[Widows Peak Conditions |Current Conditions]]. Either way will create a link that shows the text on the right while linking to the page on the left, a much easier way to change how a page looks while still linking to your intended target.

Stub Lists

When you create a link to a page that does not exist yet, you are creating a stub — a page that has yet to be created and needs to be worked on. To effectively manage stubs, most wiki engines will have a list of all stubs in the database, or all the pages that need to be completed that have not yet been worked on. It is important to maintain this list and ensure no one is creating endless stubs that are not going to be filled in anytime soon. It is a waste of time and energy in more ways than one.

Renaming Links

In some cases, you may need to rename the links that point to a certain page along with the page in question. You might think doing this would be complex, but in most cases it is quite easy and takes only a single tool. Certain wikis do it better than others, but most of them have the tool. Usually you can find it under topic actions. Then rename or move the topic and you should be able to change the page along with all the links to the page with one click. This saves a lot of time in having to go back through and change them all manually because a certain page is no longer valid in its title.

Linking to Outside URLs

When you create internal links to a wiki, the process is incredibly easy and only takes the use of a couple of tags. External links are not that much harder in that they fit into the same basic structure with only a slight change.

- A standard URL to a Web site might look like this: **www. website.com.**
- To make this into a link within a wiki, you would use this: [**www.website.com**]

There are also a slew of different ways to speed up linking between certain kinds of Web sites. For example, if you are linking to another wiki, many times major wikis are included in a predefined database within your wiki engine that allows you to simply type the name of the wiki in via Camel Case such as: [[Wikipedia:Countries_of_the_World]]

This link would tell your wiki to link to the category page in Wikipedia for Countries of the World. Similar links work for many other major wikis, including all of those in the MediaWiki network such as Wikitravel, Wiktionary, and BibleWiki.

Files, Images, and Video

When adding files, images, and videos to your wiki the process will vary slightly depending on the wiki you are using. Most wiki engines will have an uploading tool that allows you to simply up-load and add an image, video, or attachment to your server. You can then insert it directly into the wiki entry from there with any of a number of buttons on the WYSIWYG editor (see the chapter about creating a wiki for more information on the editors). If you are interested in developing a faster, easier way to do this by link-ing directly to existing files, you are going to use slightly different links than normal.

In this case, you are going to almost always use an HTML caller for the file. Attachments that you upload to your wiki are techni-cally entered into the code automatically like this for you and will usually just show up as an icon with a link to download the file automatically. Here are the HTML callers you will use for linking to outside images or files:

For Images

For an outside image, you will use the IMG SRC tag from HTML, which looks like this: <img src="file root">

In the space of the file root, you can either enter the URL of a file somewhere on the Internet or you can enter the root space of the file on your server to place an image from your own server directly into the wiki (probably a more common means of doing this).

For Files

For file attachments, you will use the classic linking A HREF tag structure from HTML: <a href="file root">Text</a>

You simply replace the text in the file root spot with the location of the attachment you would like to include and the text will appear as a link to download that file. If you are interested in adding any number of different resources here, many wiki engines will provide plug-ins or add-ons that allow visual representations or slide shows for attachments, while hosted wikis almost always have an easy, two-step process for adding them into the page.

Embedded Files

Embedded files will almost always vary depending on what they are and where you would like to add them. The HTML tag for embedding is <embed src> but in many cases, you are going to need to turn on a plug-in within your wiki engine to do this.

Every wiki engine has a different means of doing this and some of them have it automatically turned on (usually if you are using

WYSIWYG, you will have it automatically turned on), so check your engine's documentation to see if you need to turn this on manually or not. Generally though, you can simply turn on the plug-in and enter the URL of the embedded file, such as a You-Tube video. The file will then appear where you have designated in the page. For more information, see your engine or hosted wiki's help files.

Categories and Tags — Linking and Structuring

The final thing to consider in linking is how to include your pages within categories. Since most wikis are built within a very simple, open-ended platform that does not allow you to do much more than describe for the platform what the text will look like, you almost always have to manually enter the categories into the text of the wiki page. This is not always exactly the case, but you should know how to do it just in case.

Categories in a wiki are collections of pages that are defined within that category, which means that you can usually find them relatively easily by simply clicking through to the category and seeing which pages link to that category. To add a page to a category manually, use the following tag:

[[Category:CategoryName | Page Name]]

This link tells the wiki that you are creating a category link to back link to that collection of pages. You then tell it which category to back link to and what the name of the current page is that you would like to include in that category. You can enter as many of these at the bottom of the page as you like, making it easier to access and contribute pages to multiple categories.

Alternately, some wiki engines use tags instead of categories. Technically, the two are pretty much the same. You create a grouping of pages that all fit into the same basic entry and then you can look them up by that listing. Tags are a bit more versatile in that you can rank them, list them by popularity, and link to them from external resources more easily. Usually, tags need to be turned on via a plug-in from an outside resource. If you want to use tags, make sure to research the documentation on your wiki and see how it wants you to do so.

Generally speaking, you are going to find that linking within a wiki is one of the easiest navigational tasks you will ever have and that if you want to be effective in making sure your wiki is easy to navigate across the board, you will need to pay special attention to it. Although almost every time you will need to maintain a close eye on things to make sure your fellow users are following the same rules, open stubs are minimized and that content fits into the same basic structure across the board. When you start making substitutions, taking shortcuts, or sacrificing structure for speed, a wiki can become an unwieldy mess to get around.

Conclusion

While it might seem simple, linking and categorizing your wiki is one of the most important things you can do. This is because your linking and categorization will directly affect how well your wiki performs in search engines and how easy it is to get between pages in the site itself. If you are creating a content wiki or a public access community wiki, having this kind of exposure is tantamount to getting new users and building a community. If you are creating a process wiki for internal use in your organization, having the right linking and category structure will be vital to being able to find pages and keep vital project documents in the right place. Always maintain a close eye on how your linking structure is maintained to avoid the problems that many wikis have had to go through.

[[CHAPTER 9]]

Wiki Promotion

For those creating wikis on private servers and Intranet, a wiki is nothing more than a tool to use in the office, but for the rest of us, it is something that is supposed to draw visitors and support from around the Internet, and the more people you can get to show up, the better off you will be. But, are you going to be truly effective with a wiki if you do not know how to promote it? Probably not.

It is almost more important that you know how to gather new users and readers for your wiki than it is that you can create the wiki to get started. If you cannot do them both in tandem, you will find the process even longer and more arduous than you originally anticipated.

What Not to Do

The first thing you are going to need to consider is the wide slew of things you should not be doing. Why start out a chapter by throwing a list of "Do Nots" at you? It is simple — by not doing these things, you will actively promote your wiki to others and attract new users.

The Audience

The primary thing that you need to consider whenever you start any Web site, let alone a wiki, is who your audience is. You need to be 100 percent clear on who will want to see your wiki, who will want to add content, and how you can approach them to get them to do so. If you do not know who those mysterious people are, good luck tracking them down.

This can be done in any number of ways. Most people, when they start a new Web site of any type, will front it with some form of niche research. This means that they will spend some time going through various resources, reading about the topic, reading comments and text from other people who are interested in the niche, and building up a portfolio of sorts to draw from.

For the most part, you probably know your niche as well as anyone else; otherwise, why would you start a wiki about it? However, if you do not, make sure you have versed yourself in the terminology of your niche, the style of text that is written, and anything else that might be specific to your niche in any way.

The Right First Impression

Once you know your content and your audience you need to start developing your page, and the first thing anyone sees when they land on your wiki is the title. If your readers see something on the front page of your wiki like "My Wiki," they have absolutely no idea what they are looking at. In the same way that the GeoCities Web sites of the mid-1990s did not get any hits because they all started with "Check out my stuff!!!", you cannot get away with adding new editors or drawing new traffic to your wiki if you use language like "My Wiki" to describe it.

You do not need a flashy, big lettered name to draw attention; but you do need to tell your readers what your page is about. If you are developing a community wiki about Star Trek, your wiki should be at least functionally named — Star Trek Wiki — though a snappy title can go a long way in drawing additional attention and potential new people to the page. Never overlook the value humor can bring.

The Rest of That Initial Content

That does not mean you are done of course. What about the rest of the content you add to the front page of your new wiki? You had better have a very clear idea of what that content will look like, what your audience expects to see, and how to draw their attention. For example, if you are creating a blog about a television program, you had better have some images on the front page that showcase the content of the show to ensure anyone who stumbles across the page will see it. A good article sample on the front page along with a slew of good links will help to boost who sees you as well. They will see a functional, well-established wiki and be more willing to read or contribute than if they saw something that was a functional mess.

Your Organizational Structure

Finally, you need to be sure that your structure is well defined. If someone arrives on your site and cannot navigate their way through your content, good luck getting them to stick around and add to it. You need to develop a clear idea of where things go, how they should look, and when a page is unnecessary. This ontology is described more in depth in another chapter, but you need to be sure that you are ready to make adjustments if necessary to accommodate your readers.

Do Not Ignore It

This is probably one of the most commonly made mistakes with a new wiki and there is absolutely no reason for it to happen. Too many times, people will create a wiki and then expect it to flourish. The most common example of this dilemma is in the case of individuals who set up a Web site for a business or a school and then just simply expect their coworkers or students to use it. There are a few reasons why this might not work.

First of all, wikis are still relatively new technology. They are different and many people do not understand how they work or why they should work. They do not have the time or the energy to figure it out and if you are not going to help them, you can kiss having them contribute goodbye.

Second, wikis are huge prospects. They attempt to compile knowledge from multiple sources into a single database that can be edited by any of those individuals. The result is that most individuals feel like a part of the whole. However, when one person is left to their own devices, with no one else adding content or making changes, it can seem overwhelming and they give up or do not try.

You need to be involved, you need to be active with the individuals using a wiki, and you need to know how to speak to them. Make yourself available, add to the wiki yourself regularly, and contact your fellow editors with any questions, comments, or hellos you may have.

The best plan here is to ensure that before anything goes live and starts drawing traffic that you have contributed a large chunk of content to the site. Many people starting wikis will find friends who can contribute or hire out work to have a few pages filled in before it goes live. Think of it this way: Would you be more willing to add your content to a wiki that needs 1,000 pages of content and has five or a wiki that needs 1,000 pages of content and has 200? It is a huge difference and it will make a solid distinction when the site starts gathering traffic.

No Spam

Spamming is a huge problem for just about any part of the Internet, and wikis are no different. Many times, when a user creates a new Web site of any kind, they want people to visit it and they will just spam the heck out of everyone they know, the forums they visit, and the social networks they are members of. There are a few reasons why this kind of activity is a bad idea.

1. Membership Sites Do Not Like It — MySpace and Facebook, among so many others, do not like when their members spam each other about anything, even if it is in good faith. You will get your account banned and lose what little access you had to those users.
2. Google and Other Search Engines Do Not Like It — Search engines, and Google especially, will penalize you severely if you use their services to spam your Web site into the listings. It is a sure way to have your Web site blacklisted and never get any traffic.

3. Readers and Contributors Do Not Like It — No one likes to be inundated and spammed into doing anything. The spamming methods used by many do not even work that well anymore and you are going to find most people more than willing to report you rather than visit your site.

In the end, spam is borderline illegal, incredibly obnoxious, and largely useless. Do not bother with it and you will be a lot better off in the promotion of your site.

Keep it Simple

While some users may make the mistake of putting too much stock on their visitors to edit and create the wiki, others will become a bit too overzealous and take control of every aspect of the site, attempting to have editorial control over everything. You cannot do this on a wiki. It goes against everything the format stands for.

You need to be able to let the other people who visit your site edit the content and keep it under wraps. If you go in and change every new entry that users add to the site, you are going to have quite a few people moving on very quickly when they realize you are a control freak. Be willing to remit control of the content, be ready to work with others, and keep it simple.

Ignore Controversies

Controversies are only going to cause you problems if you try to integrate them into a wiki. Just visit any of a number of controversial pages on Wikipedia, such as political profiles or current events, and you will see the arguments that carry on in the comments and editing marks of the page. While this can be supported and controlled on a small scale (a few pages out of millions), consider what happens if you try to build an entire wiki out of controversial topics.

For example, a newspaper editorial staff attempted to create a wiki where users could discuss and comment on recent editorials from the newspaper. The page lasted about two days before it was removed due to the angry, confrontational comments made by multiple users. The format did not work, backfiring rapidly when the conversation escalated.

It is best to remember a few important things. People are much more willing to say something rude or humiliating on the Internet. The anonymity of the format gives them a feeling of entitlement and invincibility that interpersonal relations do not have offline. Shame and self consciousness tend to disappear in a virtual space. Keep this in mind when you create your wiki and you should be able to avoid controversy.

The Right Things

While there is a huge list of do not's that is going to hinder your operation, if you let anything get out of control, do not forget the things you should be doing as well. Sitting idly by and letting the wiki tick away is not going to draw new users. You need to get up and get out there — do some promotion. The following methods will allow you to boost the visibility of your wiki, keep users that do arrive, and cater your promotional methods to the type of wiki that you have created.

Start the Wiki

If you create a wiki, attach it to a server, and then just let it idle, it is not going to draw traffic. For this reason, you need to generate content to draw attention. This does not just make the people who might add more content to the site more willing to add that content; it allows more visibility for your wiki in search engines and cross-linking. Consider what happens whenever you type pretty much any proper noun into a search engine. Usually the first thing that appears is an entry from Wikipedia. Google especially loves informational resources, and wikis are the ultimate example. The content links to itself multiple times over, boosting SEO and making the site easy to search and spider. If you have more pages created, the content will more rapidly develop and spawn on search engines, drawing more searches and more users.

The best way to start out a wiki from scratch is to develop with a goal of hitting at least 10 percent of the content. Of course, the content you might find on a wiki might go well above what you envision, but if you think you might have 500 pages, create 50 of them to get started; it will look nicer, show your users how the site is organized, and develop SEO performance from the start.

Remove the Barriers

Wikis may be the easiest and most straightforward Web sites on the Internet to gain access to and add content to, but for the most part you are going to find that the vast majority of people do not know what they are getting into with a wiki. The simple barrier of technology can cause innumerable problems for those who would like to use wikis. They do not know how the site works, how to add content, how to develop ideas or link them together, or even how to collaborate with each other.

Education

The first thing you should do in this regard is teach your users how to use the wiki. Simple documentation is not necessarily going to cut it. While most wiki platforms have a great amount of content written on how to use them, it can go a long way to have a sandbox (if you are hosting your own) or links to a sandbox for them to practice their wiki creation skills. Additionally, you should show them how to develop and create new content in ways that are going to work on a wiki. Tell them content needs to be matched to other pages (most wikis require that you have at least two links to a new entry) and show them the quality guidelines.

Initiation

Many people will not simply start crafting content for a wiki because they feel like it is not their place. This is where you need to be sure people know that they are free to do as they please. This is vital in classroom, office, and other professional settings. If you set up a classroom wiki and tell students to add content, they may or may not know exactly what they need to include into the wiki, but for the most part, they will probably just add content to existing pages. The thought of creating content is often scary to those who have not done it before. Promote initiation and show them how to get it started.

Collaboration

Collaboration is what makes wikis so unique and is vital in preparing the highest quality content. Show users how to use the editing and comment pages as well as how to contact each other and change content. Promote careful collaboration with minimal rudeness and a general respect for each other. This will eventually roll over and create an environment in which uses are free and happy to use the format to share their ideas with each other.

Encourage Boldness

When you are trying to convince other people to get involved in a project, you need to give them incentive. This can be done in a few ways. One way, if you are a teacher trying to get students to use the wiki, is to make their grade depend on it or to offer extra credit. If you are an office manager, the job is a little easier. Workers need a paycheck and you are their boss. Exert some power. But, if you are starting a community wiki or simply want to build an informational resource, convincing people to add to your wiki is a bit harder.

One of the best ways to do this is to encourage boldness in additions. This does not mean that people should step out on a limb and start making things up when they add content to the wiki. But, it does mean that you can encourage them to provide a bit of themselves that they might not otherwise put out there without a little bit of a push. Give them incentive by allowing more creative control and they will probably be more willing to post.

Promoting Your Wikis

The act of promoting a wiki is going to be largely dependent on what kind of wiki you create and who you think will be willing to view it. Of course, the people you "need" on the wiki are your target audience with everyone else filing in after that.

Focusing in for a Community Wiki

Wikis that focus on community activities or topics need to be focused. If it is too general, you are only opening yourself up to a larger number of competitors and making it harder for your potential members to decide whether your wiki is worth existing and adding to. For that matter, they are going to want to know exactly what they get out of it. If they are looking for a wiki on rock climbing conditions and you start posting information about cycling, they might be let down at how watered down the content starts to look. Make sure to maintain your focus on the topic at hand.

Advertising

The second aspect to consider is that you need to advertise a bit. That does not mean you need to spend money to get people to see your wiki, but you need to develop some plan of sorts that will encourage individuals to visit your Web site and either read or add to it. There are a few different advertising resources out there. Here are some examples to get you started. Remember that creativity in advertising is the key to success in developing a Web site:

- **Google AdWords** — The easiest way to advertise anything is to purchase ad space in the Google search results. The ads will appear alongside searches for keywords you select and you pay a cost per click for every time a user clicks on your ad. It is highly targeted and can be very successful, but keep in mind that it can also become very expensive.
- **Link Swapping** — If you know of other wikis, blogs, or Web sites that would compliment your wiki, talk to their owners about swapping links to benefit the both of you.

You can share advertising this way and develop your search results that much faster (Google loves links from quality Web sites to yours).

- **Paid Advertising on Sites** — In the same vein, you can pay other Web sites to put a link on your page. However, keep in mind that this can hurt organic search engine positioning. If you place yourself on someone's Web site with a paid ad, the link from that page will not be counted by Google and can actually hurt any overall SEO efforts.

- **Blog Plugs** — This is a huge way to boost your promotion. Simply go to various blogs devoted to your subject and post links to your wiki in your comments. Talk to the blog owners and many times you can get them to allow guest posts. A simple 400-word post can turn into a few thousand hits to your site for only 30 minutes of your time.

There are numerous other ways to advertise your wiki as well if you are creative enough. Developing a product to sell with back-end access, creating a viral video or eBook, or simply going out and posting ads on **www.craigslist.com** will all help boost traffic among so many other methods.

What About Those Process Wikis?

Of course, straight up advertising and content development is not going to get you traffic if you are trying to jump start a process wiki. While wikis are great tools for streamlining in-house processes for teaching, office work, or any form of mass collaboration, you are going to find that getting individuals involved in your project is not nearly so easy. Here are a few ways to consider how to jump start your process wiki:

Developing Templates

If you are working in an office or classroom setting, the number one problem often ends up being a lack of technological familiarity by your audience. Students and coworkers may not know exactly what they need to do to access and use a wiki effectively. To get around this, provide templates of how a wiki page should look along with detailed instructions on how to fill in the template. If you provide the wiki coding and simply have the individuals fill in the blanks, you can save a great deal of time. Here is an example of a project listing template that would save time for a sales person who should be posting each prospective lead on to a wiki:

```
==Title of the Project==
Short Description of Prospective Project
===Timeline===
*Date of Initial Contact
*Additional Dates of Note
*Additional Dates of Note
===Contact===
*Name of Contact
*Phone Number of Contact
*[e-mail address of contact text here]
===Additional Notes===
Any Additional notes about the project go here.
```

This template is oversimplified of course. Most templates might include various tables, company specific information, and links to other projects, specific project managers, and other details of note, but the key here is that you have given them something to fill. If you inform them to leave all punctuation in place and replace all the text with their details, they can quickly and easily make an entry to the wiki without becoming confused and you have now transitioned someone into using your database.

In the Classroom

For teachers, the problem may not be quite as complex as in an office space. In most cases, technology is something that children and teens adjust to much quicker than adults, and many of them may have already used a wiki a few times — probably more often than the teacher themselves.

However, it is still vital to never assume they will understand how to use the technology. Always provide basic documentation and a simple, straightforward purpose for each template. If you want your students to post their class projects to a wiki and collaborate with their group members there, you will need to describe to them an etiquette guide to go along with the templates so they know what is appropriate and what is not.

Additionally, many classroom wikis have trouble with organization. One of the best ways to get around this problem is to assign a single student to track changes in a group. Have them be in charge of organizing pages, cleaning up the markup, and compiling the project when it is completed. It will create a sense of responsibility in someone that will affect their grade and if something happens, such as vandalism, they will likely inform you before the project becomes ruined.

Access in the Classroom

Another problem that many teachers face in the new age of computers in every classroom, home, and library is that not every student always has access to a computer. Many schools today are providing laptops to their students, and computer labs are common around the country, but if your school does not provide these things, always consider the access your students have to the Internet. If they cannot regularly log on to the Internet and access a wiki, they may not be able to participate.

Building from Top Down

If you want a group of peers to adopt a new technology, you need to build from the top down. This means that in an office setting, you need to be sure that the man or woman at the top of the totem pole is using the wiki technology before you can expect the guys in the mail room to use it. Otherwise, you are probably wasting resources. Start at the top and ensure it trickles down.

The same goes for in the classroom where the teacher leads the way in many cases. You will need to provide resources via the wiki, work with the students, and regularly update from and access the wiki if you expect your students to do the same.

If you create a wiki that does not work from the top of the totem pole down to the bottom, you are going to have a slew of individuals who are not only bored with the resource, but that will question why they need to be involved in it at all. Make sure that you are an integral part of every operation that occurs on your wiki and that you are ready for just about everything that is added to it. If a new section is added, you do not necessarily need to change anything, but make sure to read it. The second you start falling out of the loop on what is happening on your wiki is the second it starts to scale out of your control. At this point you need to start rethinking things like how to maintain it, who can help you gauge its growth, and how to slow it down or stop it.

Other Promotional Methods

While most of the information in this chapter covers in fairly vivid detail everything you need to know about how to develop a wiki and start to get people to use it, there are a few things that are not specific to any one wiki — and which mainly focus on things related to content and community wikis that will use search engines and Internet resources to attract and develop user bases.

For the most part, you will be using search engine optimization or SEO techniques to develop how effective your wiki will perform in the various search engines on many levels. Most SEO techniques will work directly with Google because it is the largest search engine with nearly 70 percent of all search volume and because it has the strictest ranking algorithms. Simply put, if you can do well in Google, you will probably do well in the other search engines. In this section you will learn a few basic methods that many people use to boost their search engine rankings for certain topics and keywords. Keep in mind, however, that an entire book could be written about SEO and it still would not be complete. These are just simple things to get you started in the mindset of what it will take to effectively promote your Web site.

Link Building

The crux of Google's search rankings is based on links you receive from other Web sites. To put it in simple terms, Google views each link you get as a vote. However, unlike a standard democracy, each vote is weighted. The better a Web site is, the more weight its vote has. You have probably seen those page rank numbers before on some Web sites and wondered what they had to do with anything. It is not an easy task to break down the entire page rank formula, but to put it simply, this is the level of importance that Google places on your site. If you have a page rank of six, you are more important than a Web site with a page rank of four.

What this means for you, with your shiny new wiki, is that when you get a link from a Web site with a higher page rank, your own ranking will go up just that much more. So, your goal is going to be to get as many high quality links as possible. The hard part of course is getting those Web sites to put your link on their Web site.

How a Link Needs to Look

In addition to those links, you need to be sure they are properly structured. It means that they need to be keyword anchored. Google will look at what text is used to describe a link to know what your Web site is about and what it should show up for in searches. If someone links to your Web site with the text "Jim's Wiki," then you will have that much higher of a chance to show up in Google when someone types "Jim's Wiki" as a search query.

So, when you get your links listed on other Web sites, you need to strive to get them listed with the right anchor text describing keywords for your Web site. If you do not do this, you are not going to get the right quality links. You will be wasting valuable linking opportunities and while your overall page rank might increase, you still will not appear in Google for the keywords you need to show up for.

What Are the Right Keywords?

This brings us to our next point of interest — what keywords should you be focusing on? The right keywords are going to be the ones that are focused directly on your subject matter without being too highly competitive with other Web sites and that have enough room for growth to draw large numbers of traffic.

A good way to start is to develop a list of the words and phrases that describe your wiki. Now, start researching those phrases simply by typing them into Google. What appears when you type in those keywords? If there are 2,000,000 matches, it is a good bet that you are going to have some competition. Now, look at the top few links that appear. These are your top competitors. You may never beat them, but that is the benchmark for the keyword. If the site has 1,000 links to it from quality Web sites, you are going to have a hard time getting people to see your own site.

Good Web sites for further keyword research are Wordtracker and Keyword Discovery. They are both paid services but come with free trials that allow you to enter a keyword into their database and view the search volume of that keyword across multiple different databases along with a list of similar keywords you may not have considered for your needs. Basically, if you want to search for "rock climbing," it would tell you that the key phrase gets 65,000 hits a month on average and that competition is very high for it. You could then look at other related keywords like "rock climbing routes" or "rock climbing conditions" and find that competition is lower without the search volumes going down too much.

This type of basic research will be the crux of how you start your optimization efforts and will involve a lot of trial and error. Luckily, you do not have to worry about optimizing your actual content for any reason. A wiki is one of the most keyword rich Web sites on the Internet for whatever topic it happens to be about. Because a wiki links back to itself hundreds or even thousands of times, has dozens of titles per topic, and reuses keywords constantly, it will jump straight up in terms of keyword density and volume quickly.

Methods of Boosting Search Rankings

The actual methods used to boost your links from other Web sites and start to appear higher in search rankings start with a simple run through of the different ways in which you can get those links on quality Web sites. Keep in mind that any method that is considered spam will only hurt you more than help. Google is very keen on picking up and blacklisting any URL that spams its listings. So, you need to be legitimate but that does not mean you cannot push the results along a little faster.

Article Posting

Articles can be written and posted to directories like **http:// ezinearticles.com** where they will be listed for free to republish for use by other Web sites. Those other links are meaningless. However, the link you get from the article directories, which often have page ranks as high as six or seven, are worth a great deal. You need to mix up your linking text back to your site, and use as many high-ranked article directories as you can to be effective here.

The quality of the articles does not need to be high, but one thing you will find is that the higher quality you write, the more likely you are going to perform well in terms of SEO. Google's natural language algorithms and ability to recognize poorly written content is getting better every day it seems and the longer they are around, the less likely it is that Web sites or articles written solely for ranking in their index will show up very high.

Blog Posting and Promotion

Contacting blog owners who have highly ranked blogs with lots of links is a great way to boost your rankings. Offer to write free posts, offer to swap links, or simply start commenting often and you will benefit from their high rankings when they point back to you. Blogging is one of the most effective means of social promotion on the Internet today and for a few good reasons. First of all, you have a resource that works almost entirely within the sphere of word of mouth. People are interested in a blog so they comment on it, link to it, or put it in their feed. It then spreads to other feeds, shows up in sites like Technorati, or simply jumps up in search engines and while the content does not need to be all that technical, useful information about a specific topic can drive the popularity of your site up even further.

Effectively Writing Article or Blog Posts

Writing articles and blog posts for search engine ranking boosts is vital to getting the necessary backlinks to your Web site when it is new. Your wiki will undoubtedly perform well on its own eventually, but you want to get some highly needed traffic coming in right away so that you can build a community of users and start growing. However, poorly written articles and blog posts will not get you anywhere.

To start with, you need to work with topics that are related to your wiki's content without being overtly promotional. Trying to sell your wiki in an article will not get you very far. There are a few reasons for this. First, search engines do not like self-aggrandizing content. Second, article directories tend to turn submissions down when they are overtly promotional. Third, no one wants to read a blog that does not have actual information they can use.

To get around these points and to create quality content, write like you would for your wiki, only with a bit more personality. Create quality, informational content with your personal touch added to ensure it is more engaging than a boring article in a wiki or an eye roll, inducing sales pitch. Make sure to inject keywords naturally into the text, using them at no more than 4 percent density for casual SEO and never ruining grammar just for the sake of getting in keywords. If you remember these things and find topics you enjoy writing about, it will show in your finished products and will get you better results for both article submissions and blog posts.

Social Networks and Bookmarking

Web sites like Facebook and MySpace can help build links as well. The links from these sites are minimally effective, but the links you can gather from feeds and aggregates of the sites are very helpful. You can also use sites like Twitter, Digg, and StumbleUpon to bookmark listings and develop additional links back to your site.

Facebook

Facebook is not the largest social network out there (MySpace still holds that designation), but it is the most effective and the highest quality. If you want to develop an effective plan to sell your wiki to contacts and friends, Facebook has more tools, a better interface, and a more mature audience and that all makes for a great resource for you. Create not only a personal page to connect with new friends, but also a page on which you can develop a following for your wiki alone.

Twitter

Twitter is a tool that allows users to produce a short little blurb to a feed that other users can subscribe to. They can follow your Twitter to see how you are doing on Monday morning or to see when you have posted a new page on your wiki. This is a valuable tool that you can tie into an RSS feed so users will constantly know when your wiki is updated and when they can go check it out. They might do it simply out of boredom in many cases. Never underestimate the power of boredom.

Digg

Digg is a tool that allows users to vote on Web sites that are submitted to the service. If someone likes a page, they Digg it. This produces a free link on the Digg Web site that either rises or falls depending on how many people Digg it and how many visits it gets.

Delicious

This is a shared bookmarking service on which people can post their own listing of bookmarks and search through each other's to find popular sites, top new services, and much more. Get your wiki listed in as many Delicious accounts as possible and you can boost your visibility many times over with numerous new links.

List Building and Recruiting

While it does not fit directly into SEO, one tool that many Web site owners use is to directly promote themselves to their potential customers by creating mailing lists or contact forms that those potential customers opt into. Individuals who may not be fully interested in a topic will read useful information that is sent to their e-mail address along with a single link each day, week, or month (depending on how often you mail them) to visit your wiki.

The key here is that they must show interest before you can contact them. Simply sending out e-mails to random individuals is considered spam and will ultimately result in your e-mail address and wiki being blacklisted and dropped from the search engines.

A good way to start doing this is to create a simple mailing list that you place on your wiki somewhere. Advertise it by telling visitors that they can get updates every set amount of time you want to mail them — bi-weekly or weekly is recommended — with information related to the wiki's content. If you are creating a rock climbing wiki, tell them you will include condition updates once a week. If you are creating a video game wiki, send tips or tricks out once a week. Whatever you decide to do, make

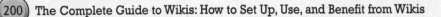

sure it is a valuable piece of information that they will want to read and that will draw them back to the Web site.

While this tactic is generally used to sell products, it can work just as well for your wiki, which is essentially a sale of its own. Instead of selling information or products though, you are trying to sell something much more valuable — a volunteer opportunity to fill in content on your wiki. If users start returning after reading your e-mails, they will find more content on your wiki and will eventually, if they read enough, start adding their own updates to the page.

When properly integrated, this is a solid tactic that will help boost the visibility of almost any Web site. Just remember to be wary of anything that even borders on spam-like tactics. You will regret the consequences if you get too aggressive.

Smart SEO Will Make or Break Your Wiki

A good wiki that relies on Web traffic needs to perform in the search engines. You cannot be effective off of word of mouth alone. So, for that reason, you are going to need to be effective with your SEO off the bat. In the long run, if people add new content regularly and your wiki grows, it will show up high in search rankings. But, if you want it to continue to remain high and especially if you want those rankings right away, you are going to need to get some solid traffic right away and SEO is the best way to do so organically and for free.

There are countless resources out there that will detail in wide, sweeping action plans how you can develop your SEO strategy and develop a Web site that will be visited by hundreds if not thousands of people a day without you paying a single dime to do it.

[[CHAPTER 10]]

Wiki Security
and Management

Now that you have a slew of new people scouring your wiki, adding information, editing old articles, and contributing to your new corner of the Internet, how do you keep the wiki both clean and safe? For that matter how do you keep it well organized against the threat of online vandalism, assault, and other possible issues that are all but sure to pop up?

It is not just a matter of protecting your time investment — it is a responsibility to those people who use your wiki and have contributed their time and knowledge to it — to make sure that you secure and maintain the safety of your wiki at all costs. You cannot let it grow weak in the face of attacks by vandals or hackers or simply to fall apart without proper maintenance. This is a part of the process.

Potential Threats

The first thing you need to do in protecting your wiki is to understand what threats you might face. It does you no good to try and protect something if you have no idea what might happen that requires protection. Here are a few things that commonly occur online and to wikis especially that you can help to prevent.

Vandalism

Vandalism is going to happen, especially if your goal is to have open collaboration on your wiki. The more open you make a Web site the more often it is going to be messed with by various users and the more likely you are going to need to go in and make changes. For a good idea of how to handle vandalism, let us take a look at how Wikipedia, a site that has thousands of edits every hour, handles vandalism on the grand scale that it invites.

To start with, Wikipedia has a group of dedicated users that works only to go through the list of changes that are made to Wikipedia regularly and check to see if any of them are illegitimate. Many of them are and using the tools integrated into Wikipedia for these high-end volunteers, they can go through and remove all changes made by single individuals (since registration is required) and roll back pages that were vandalized.

You are going to see things like advertising for sites, SEO hijacking (creating links back to their own sites), clever jokes, and goofy segues. For example, Stephen Colbert of "The Colbert Report" on Comedy Central asked his audience on an episode in 2007 to go onto Wikipedia and change the page for elephants to say they were no longer endangered. The page was changed numerous times back and forth as millions logged in and tried to change. The volunteers at Wikipedia kept a close eye on the page though and maintained it throughout all those changes.

You are going to need a safeguard similar to how Wikipedia operates to allow you the freedom and control needed to safely and quickly remove vandalism from your site.

Hardware Problems

A major issue that can affect your wiki is the server and system on which it is running. If you run a computer program on a machine, it will eventually have problems. People who prepare for these problems are much less likely to have concerns when they occur. Of course, if you create a wiki through a hosted service, you will have much less to worry about than most people because the hosting service backs up content and performs regular maintenance.

However, if you run your own server or have a VPS account somewhere, make sure that you regularly perform maintenance and back up everything on your server so it cannot be lost. This is a good practice no matter where your wiki is. That is a whole lot of work to just go up and missing one day if there is a disc error or the server gets destroyed or something.

Malicious Attacks

It does not happen often unless you have something that invites attack, but you need to be wary of any instance in which you could draw the ire or attention of a hacker or malicious attack on your

Web site. Wikis tend not to see much of this because they are so easily vandalized and do not require fancy break-ins, but it does happen and if you are not prepared for it with quality security software and backups of everything that you have on your server, you are going to have further problems almost every time.

Useless Changes

While it might not be a security problem, you are going to have people who get carried away and want to add their personal "slant" to everything they see. They will go into countless pages and make arbitrary changes that just do not need to exist. This is another good reason for having a secure listing of all the editorial guidelines and a means by which to ensure everyone that makes changes can be tracked and those changes can be rolled back if necessary.

Keep in mind, however, that if the changes made by the user were in good faith, you should consider keeping them around and offering them something they can do with all that enthusiasm. Point them to the tutorials, show them how to make useful changes, and ensure they have a category or role that they can fill without causing trouble throughout your wiki. Everyone you can get on your side is a useful addition to your team.

Anger and Controversy

A wiki is an open forum more than anything else and because of that, you invite anyone from anywhere to enter the site and write whatever they want about whatever they want. The problem that develops here is that sometimes topics or content is highly sensitive and you are going to have a great deal of argument and anger that sparks if you do not tamp it down quickly. It can lead to vandalism or worse if you are not careful.

For example, any page that contains content considered high risk for passionate responses on Wikipedia is littered with warnings for anyone that makes edits or uses the discussion page to talk about possible changes. Things like gay marriage, the Iraq war, and abortion will have warnings telling people not to discuss anything of a personal nature, no opinions, no changes without talking about them first, make sure everything has a reference, etc. Sometimes things will slip through these warnings and people will incite others, but if you want to have topics that will draw anger and controversial responses from different sides, make sure you put safeguards in place beforehand.

Keeping Track of Changes and Spam

One of the biggest things you need to be able to do is to effectively track changes and any spam that might come through to your wiki as it comes in. A good system set in place, run by a few dedicated staff members that regularly go through the recent changes list and make sure they are all in good faith, can be an invaluable tool in maintaining your wiki throughout any major problems that might arise.

However you decide to develop your group of volunteers, make sure they are both trustworthy and effective in their work. If they

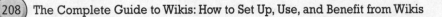

are likely to make mistakes themselves or hold grudges, they may not be good for such an impartial role in your wiki.

Versions and Rolling Back Changes

When an unwanted change is made to your wiki, you have a few options. First, you can roll back the page to a previous version that was not a problem. This is possible in every wiki engine out there as they will all keep track of specific versions as marked and agreed upon by the users that create the content.

To find these versions, you can click on the History tab that appears atop pretty much every wiki engine out there. When you do this, you will have access to the different versions of the page and when they were edited. Each edit ever made will be listed and in most cases you can sort them by major and minor edits (minor edits are usually marked as such when someone makes a change to the page).

You can also compare the versions by looking at the markup on the versions (most wikis save a cache of all those old versions). Usually green and red text will be used to show you what was added or deleted from the page when changes were made. All text that appears that was not highlighted is part of both versions of the page and will stay the same no matter what.

Once you find the version that you like and that was the last effective version before the vandalism or misguided changes, you can roll back the page to that version. You should also add a comment here as most engines allow you to do so that you can tell anyone else that comes along why you rolled the page back. If you explain that it was vandalism, no one will need to double check to ensure your rollback is not vandalism as well.

In some cases you will not be able to simply restore to an old version. If this is the case, copy and paste the old version of the page (the wiki should still store the old versions even if it will not allow you to rollback) and then replace the newer version.

If you make a rollback change, you need to be sure that the changes you make are not only correct but that the newer version of the page does not include anything of actual value. For example, if someone made a trio of changes and one of the three seems like a good change while the other two are frivolous, you should simply delete the other two manually instead of rolling the page back and destroying the good change that was made. Another option here is to bring it up on the discussion page where other users can go over changes and what may or may not be considered a good change.

Recent Changes Tracking

While being technically capable of rolling back the changes that have been made to a wiki in error or malice is vital to effectively operating a wiki, the second important thing you will need to focus on is being able to keep close eyes on the recent changes that are made to your wiki. It does you no good to know how to make changes to vandalism or mistakes if you do not pay enough attention to notice when these things occur.

On any wiki you operate, whether it is an installed engine or a hosted service, you are going to have access to a page that allows you to see the most recent changes made to your wiki. Usually the page is located in the left hand navigation bar and will show you what you need to know about who has recently accessed and edited the content on your page. This list of changes should be checked every day by the group of individuals that you recruit to work on monitoring all of the changes made to your content. If they log on and check this list every day, you will always have a small but dedicated group that will make sure no changes are malicious in nature.

Notifications

Another of the more valuable tools you have at your disposal is the ability to have your wiki notify you whenever a major change is made to the content. By setting up e-mail notifications for content as it is edited so that anyone who needs to monitor specific pages can see what has been altered, someone is always able to see what needs to be done. This is especially useful for controversial topics or for content that is being proctored such as in a classroom wiki.

What to Watch For

There are plenty of things that can happen to a wiki that will cause problems if you do not act quickly to stomp them out. There are people who will gladly log into your wiki and actively strive to change anything they disagree with. There are others who will simply find humor in causing trouble within your wiki, changing things for the sake of changing things. There are others still who mean well and will make honest mistakes because they think they know more about a topic than they really do.

All three of these scenarios will probably happen to you if you operate an open wiki and all three have different responses. You are going to want have your group of editors and monitors watching for any content that does not conform to the following:

- **Quality Guidelines** — Your wiki should have a certain level of quality that it maintains throughout each page. This includes things like grammar, spelling, sentence structure, etc. If changes are made that are extremely poorly written, you will need to decide if you want your editors to delete them or to rewrite them to conform. In some cases, such as for a classroom or a business, it might not even matter if such changes are made.

- **Editorial Guidelines** — Editorial guidelines are more about the content itself. If a change is made to your wiki that does not adhere to things like how the content is supposed to be formatted, what sources are included, or what the content discusses, you may decide changes are in order. It is good to decide early on how many outside sources you will require, what kind of content you will monitor for errors, and how carefully you will engage your users to ensure they maintain these levels of quality.

- **Topic Adhesion** — Changes should always be made in the right pages. If someone adds information about Pluto to a page about a new DVD that just hit the market, they either were not paying attention to the page they were editing or their logic for how that content belonged there was a little stretched. Either way, watch out for content that ends up in the wrong place. Another possible problem here is duplication. Make sure that no content is placed on a page in duplication of another page.

- **Obvious Vandalism** — There are certain signs that will pop up that point to obvious vandalism. Make sure to watch for them. These can include slang, swearing, negative connotations, or just outright lies about a subject.

- **Facts Not Agreed Upon** — There are certain instances when a fact will be placed into a wiki entry that is not true or is not generally agreed upon. This is where the discussion page can come in handy. In these instances, it is best to roll back such changes and introduce them to the discussion page where users can get into a conversation about whether that change is warranted and if so, what resources can be used to support it.

Selective Access

One of the more valuable tools you have in most wikis (but not all of them) is the ability to control who has access to content. This is a very important aspect of controlling content and making sure that not anyone can login and edit something of importance to you or your organization. There is an ethical dilemma here that many wiki owners will encounter at some point in the lifespan of their wikis.

To start with, you will need to decide when and how to limit access. If you are operating a process wiki where you need to ensure outside sources do not login and interrupt your processes, this is a no-brainer. Teachers should limit access to the classroom and businesses should limit access to the office. However, a content wiki is a different matter. Do you really want to cut off access to certain pages in your wiki because you are unsure that the general public is capable of being selective with how they respond to parts of your content? It is a major sticking point for many wikis and one that the owner of any given wiki will need to face.

If you do decide to limit access, you can usually decide between one of two or three options — limiting it to read only where no one outside your wiki members can edit anything or limiting both reading and writing so only wiki members can see or edit the content.

Backing Up Your Content

A wiki is a huge time investment. It might take days, weeks, or even years to complete the content on one and if you are not prepared for what might go wrong, you may end up in a big hole when something crashes, vandalism over takes your system, or your server has issues. That is why all respectable wiki software and hosting services provide backup services that allow you to download the entire contents of your wiki in any number of formats.

On Wikispaces for example you can download a zip, tgz, or HTML file that will help you keep track of your wiki entries and ensure none of the content you and your members have been working so hard on gets lost.

Regular Backup Schedule

One of the best ways to maintain your content is to establish and maintain a regular backup schedule. You should be careful to set up and work with your members to maintain this schedule every set period of time. If you decide that it needs to happen each Wednesday or every odd numbered day of the week, either make sure that you are available to do it or that someone else in your team can do so. One server crash and you will openly regret not having made the decision to do so.

If you have your own wiki engine, make sure to either educate yourself on the technology behind the software or to work with someone in the tech staff for your hosting company or a friend who can help you to maintain your backups regularly. If you build a large enough wiki and plan on hiring someone to help out with the technical aspects (or are installing one in your business and have an IT person available) make sure this is something they are well versed in and can do regularly.

Conclusion

Your wiki is going to become incredibly valuable to you over time. The amount of energy and hours you will put into it will guarantee that vandalism, breakdowns in security, or hardware problems cause you more stress than anything else in your life when you first encounter them. However, by effectively preparing yourself for these problems, because they will occur, you can steel yourself to weather the storms that all wiki owners face. Be ready, backup often, and do not let small-time vandals get to you.

[[CHAPTER 11]]

Wiki Installation and Management

There are so many different aspects of a wiki on the technical side that many times new users get more bogged down with them than they do the maintenance and management of the project. If you truly want to be effective with your wiki, you need to be sure that you can maintain the site and install it properly.

The engine you install, the maintenance of the new technology, having a good crew on board, and making sure you have a well-oiled maintenance schedule in place is incredibly important.

Installing the Wiki Engine

The first thing you are going to want to know about is how to get your wiki engine up and running. There are multiple options out there and each of them is going to be a time-consuming, energy-sapping one if you do not have the right information to help you get started. Up until recently, it was not easy enough for most everyday people to install and use a wiki. They were complex, bulky things that required knowledge of multiple programming languages and server details to be able to install in the first place. However, with recent developments in how wikis operate and how they fit into place, you can do it yourself with a little bit of help and a whole lot of preparation.

The Hosting Service

The first thing to do is find the hosting service you will use for your wiki. This is a very important decision as not every hosting service is the same. You need to consider factors such as the reliability of the service you are working with, the people who are involved in its maintenance, and how effective they are at getting things done.

We will assume that you have already decided that your particular situation warrants an installed wiki versus a hosted wiki. If this is still unclear to you, go back to previous chapters and review your options. Do not forget that there are a variety of different options out there that allow you to start and operate a wiki on an existing platform with zero technical expertise. However, if you know you need the added security and control that an installed wiki provides, continue.

There are multiple different sites out there that will provide you with the resources you need to host your Web site. For any one of them you will have two options: Either a shared hosting account or a dedicated hosting account. In most cases a shared account will be plenty for what you are doing, but there may be certain situations where you need a shared account. Here is a breakdown of what each has to offer and how to make your decision a little easier:

Shared Hosting — Shared hosting is when you rent space on a server that has multiple other Web sites on it as well. You will have full access to a control panel that provides details about your account, root access, and file information, but the maintenance and complex server related stuff is taken care of by the hosting company. These accounts are usually cheaper and a little less intensive technically. If you have a small Web site that you only need to be able to control in the most basic ways, this is a great option. Make sure to find a service that will work with you and has high marks for customer service as any technical things you need completed will need to be done through customer service.

Dedicated Hosting — A dedicated host is a much more elaborate and technically advanced option for someone who is starting their own Web site. To start with, you will get your own server or your own dedicated chunk of a server cluster, which means you have root access to the files in that server, control over when it starts and stops, and what all gets installed on it. However, these accounts are much more expensive and generally require a great deal more technical expertise as you are fully responsible for everything that happens (short of hardware failure) on your server. If you plan on running a very large Web site that uses up large chunks of resources, you should choose this method.

Between the two, almost everyone reading this can probably use a shared hosting account and be alright. You want to be sure that you have enough resources for the site you are operating, but also that you do not overpay for something you do not need. If you do decide to go with a dedicated server, make sure you have someone on staff who is capable of operating and maintaining the back end where installations, complex maintenance, and troubleshooting are all done by you.

All-in-One Solutions

There are options out there for those who do not have someone on staff who can work on their wiki to sign up for an all-in-one service that will install your wiki on a server, and then offer consulting and technical service whenever you have a problem. Web sites like XWiki or MediaWiki both provide such services, allowing you to have a wiki automatically installed onto a new server account that you can then ask for help with as you need it. These services are much more expensive than standard Web services but if your wiki project is big enough and requires a more sound approach, it can be a good option.

What Your Wiki Requires

The next thing you need to do is be sure that the wiki engine you are about to install matches up with your server's technical specs. Almost all wiki engines will provide detailed technical documentation about what you will need to effectively operate the software on your server. You will need to know things like the Pearl version required, RCS, GNU, Cron Scheduler, and Web Server. Usually you can find details about these things on the technical resources page of any server hosting company, or you can e-mail their support staff and ask them if a certain wiki engine will run on their servers.

There will also be certain hardware requirements that most modern server companies will easily match. Due to increased demand from video sharing and images, most servers have been upgraded to the point that they can easily handle high volumes of text. However, keep in mind that if you expect large volumes of traffic, most shared hosting accounts are not built to handle the influx of traffic that is likely to occur when you start gathering members and readers to your wiki.

Because there will be plenty of technical details thrown at you during this phase, here is a breakdown of what each of the requirements of most wiki engines means:

Perl — This is as programming language that is used to write many wiki engines. How it works and what it provides is less important than ensuring you have the right version installed. You will find that most wiki engines will run on version 5.6.1 or higher, though some might require a slightly higher version.

CPAN Modules — These modules are specific programs that are written in Perl that allow your server to do certain things. Many software programs will use modules that are already installed on a server to save them time in programming. This can easily be the case for your wiki engine (as it is for common installations like TWiki), so be sure that all modules are installed. Most shared hosting plans will have the complete CPAN Library installed for your use.

Linux — The vast majority of installed software assumes that your server is running on Linux or Unix. This is because these two operating systems are much more stable than a Windows operated server. Most servers will be built on Linux or Unix, but make sure beforehand that this is the case. Even if your wiki engine states that it can operate on Windows, it will run less effectively and take a whole lot more work to install.

Apache — Apache is the basis by which your server operates, accepting requests for pages and sending them back to Web browsers. Pretty much everything uses Apache these days and your Web server will almost assuredly be run on it to match up with your software needs.

The Right Requirements

These are just a few examples of the various software components that your wiki may need to operate. There are other wiki engines and each of them is written in a different set of coding languages, server requirements, and details. Make sure to pick a set of software components that you not only understand (or can hire someone that understands), but that you have installed on your Web server already.

The Installation Process

Installing a wiki engine can range in difficulty from uploading an installer and filling in basic information about your server and wiki to having to physically go in and edit various bits and pieces on your server's backend. For that reason, you are going to need to spend some time learning the basics of the installation process and ensuring you have everything you need in place.

Most wiki engines will come with installation guides that are available on the Web site of the wiki. You will find detailed instructions written as simply as possible to help you install your software, but they still may be a bit too complicated for someone without knowledge of the software. For this reason, make sure to have a few resources on hand to help you out. You can go to the support Web site or forums of the wiki engine's creators where other users gather to ask and answer questions, you can hit up technical support for your hosting company, or you can contact other users via chatting services or mailing lists where you will find a slew of people willing to help you out with the finer details of your wiki installation.

Make sure to read through all documentation and installation guidelines thoroughly before asking questions of fellow users though. There is an unspoken rule on the Internet that if you ask questions before doing the research, you will not be well received. There are a lot of people out there asking questions and asking ones that have already been answered elsewhere only clogs up the lines.

At the Web site of the wiki engine you are trying to install, you should find the binaries needed to install your wiki. These are basic pieces of software and installation modules that you will use to get the wiki set up on your server. How they come packed will vary from wiki to wiki. Some, like MediaWiki, are very simple installations with a few basic files to upload and set up (it is actually a very large number of files, but they install easily). Others, like TWiki, are downloaded in sets of binaries through Zip or

TGZ (Zip for Windows and TGZ for Linux) that you will upload and unpack to install.

After downloading the files for your server, you should connect to your server and get the installation started. This is the really complicated part in some ways and is where having a trained professional on hand can help immensely. Because the actual method of connecting to the Web server and redirecting your software to look at the wiki engine can often be a very complex process, it cannot be covered in its entirety in this book.

For MediaWiki this process can be handled from an installation page that comes with the software. For TWiki it requires reformatting the http.conf file in your server's root. Whatever it requires, make sure to read your documentation carefully or contact a profession who can help you get to the next step.

Configuring Your Wiki

Once you have set up the wiki files on your server to display in your Web browser you will be able to start configuration of those files. Some wikis will require you do the configuration at the command line in your Linux Server installation, but the larger ones with more users and a lot of resources invested into them will allow you to do it through your Web browser.

After entering the URL of the configuration script and getting into the basic configuration menus that will allow you to get started, you will need to start putting a few details in so your wiki knows how to look, act, and feel when someone visits it.

In some cases you will need to set up a MySQL PHP database. This can be done on most servers through the cPanel interface. Go through the MySQL wizard to create a new database and make sure to add yourself as a new user. Then write down the information you created for that new database including the database name, the user name, server location, and port (usually these are "local" and "21"). If you do not need a MySQL database for your wiki, skip this step.

Upon returning to the configuration step for your wiki, you may need to review a few of the following bits of information before your wiki will be up and ready to run:

- **Administrator** — You should enter your name, e-mail address, and password as the administrator of the wiki. This information will allow you to log back into this page later so that you can make basic changes to the interface if necessary.

- **Path Settings** — This will tell the server where to put the wiki. It will allow you to detail where scripts are located, where the wiki files are located, and what URL users need to enter to visit your wiki.

- **Security Changes** — Each wiki has different security options. Some, like MediaWiki, have almost no options here to work with at all. Others, like TWiki, will allow you to change a number of options as you set up your software. The information here will affect how user names are handled, how user authentication is handled, and how passwords and page access is handled.

- **Anti-Spam** — Some wikis will have anti-spam software installed that allows them to monitor and alert you to any potential spam or vandalism being done to your site.

- **Language and Location** — Sometimes you may want your wiki to localize to a different language than the default (usually English). Many wiki engines will come with between three and ten languages installed for your use. Use this option to change the language.

- **Storage Settings** — This will be available for more advanced wiki installations, allowing you to change where the wiki is stored, how the files are stored, and what you will be able to access, back up, and move as the wiki progresses.

- **Mail and Alerts** — You can manage and control mail settings here and how your wiki will interface with you as the administrator. If you want alerts sent to you every time something is changed, this is where you make those adjustments to start with. You will be able to access administrator controls later as well to make changes to this.

- **Plug-ins** — Many wikis allow you to install multiple different types of plug-ins these days, putting different functions and software options into play for your wiki as your uses evolve. See the home page of your wiki to know if plug-ins are viable options for you.

Completion and Starting

Once you have set up all of your configuration settings (and there may be additional settings that are put into place by your wiki engine), you should be ready to start creating content for that wiki. Remember to save and protect the password you created as it will be used repeatedly to maintain and update your wiki as it grows.

Maintaining the Wiki

Once you have a wiki up and running, you need to start worrying about details that you may not have realized existed before. This includes things like basic maintenance of your wiki, ensuring that nothing goes wrong, and that your content is regularly checked, double checked, and backed up. A few of these points have been discussed already throughout the book, but a much more detailed, more specific outline can help to get anyone started on the road to effective wiki management.

Wikis are going to grow. They are going to get bigger and bigger and eventually are going to require a keen eye and a steady hand to cut them back down to size. Being able and willing to do this is a huge part of properly maintaining your wiki and ensuring that it keeps running smoothly at all times.

If your ontology does not work properly or your users decide to start creating pages out of nothing, the basis of the entire wiki will start to fall apart. Why does it matter if the wiki starts to get too big? This can be a problem in many ways because content starts to overlap, it starts to fall out of sequence, and it starts to fail to show up in search engines where proper linking, careful placement, and effective planning make all the difference in placement.

Your Tasks

As the wiki owner, you need to know what it is that you are expected to do. Wikis are unique creations in that you get to do less than most Web site owners because it is a community operated and owned Web site. However, if you are not careful and let too much of the work fall to others, you may end up with a messy, overgrown wiki in no time flat. So, here are a few basic tasks that each wiki owner should see to every day as they maintain their wiki:

- **Structuring and Organization** — You should be in charge of deciding if anything needs to be moved, reorganized, or just plain deleted. While content creation and management should be open ended to everyone, this is a managerial task and as the owner and the person who spends the most time on your wiki, it is best if you take on this role.

- **Training Your Users** — Make sure that your users and members are well trained and even pick a few select users to help you prune and cut down the wiki to size when needed. You may be in charge of those organizational decisions, but it can be a great idea to have a few people on hand to help you with the hard stuff.

- **Checking Changes** — This is a major aspect of all wiki maintenance and ideally a few people will be helping you with it. Make sure that someone is always checking recent changes and maintaining a close eye on all vandals, bad additions, or just plain mistakes that might sneak through the wiki and into the content.

- **Regular Maintenance** — While the content is vital, there are a ton of small, technical tasks that need to be done regularly. This means performing server maintenance, resetting your software occasionally, backing up all of your files every week or so, and generally just keeping an eye on how things are operating.

Pruning Your Wiki Effectively

To effectively prune your wiki, you need to go in with a good plan and be sure that you are ready to make the hard decisions that it takes to maintain effective wiki structure. A wiki can quickly go from useful to messy and confusing if you allow every page created to remain in place (and there will be a good number of messy additions that do not make sense, you can count on that).

On the other side of things, you may see plenty of spots where content is missing and those spaces need to be filled as quickly as possible. The longer you have empty spaces and missing content in your wiki, the longer you will have users who walk away scratching their heads, wondering if they somehow missed the point. Encourage additions, add content yourself, and make sure that empty spots do not stay that way for long.

Making Changes

There are a few ways to go about making changes or deleting content on your wiki page. You may want to establish a policy for what works best. In some cases, you might be stuck with a particular policy due to your workspace and what they have to say about maintaining data, backing up content, and deletions.

Marking Up Changes

You may want to markup your changes by using HTML tags that display when changes are made instead of simply deleting or editing the content out. A simple strike through tag, <s>, will show anyone that views a page that something was deleted without actually deleting the content. It can become a bit messy so it is generally not recommended for anything that is content related, but if you are running a project management or classroom wiki and small changes need to be made, this is a good way to go about doing so without completely removing content from a page (and without having to worry about rollbacks).

Cutting Content

This is the more common method of removing old content from a wiki in the same fashion that sites like Wikipedia use. Instead of cutting out content with strikethrough tags or highlighting, you can use basic pruning techniques to cut back the content a bit by deleting things that are unnecessary, combining pages, or removing entire sections.

Make sure to check with the author before major editing is made. They may just need to update the page a bit to make it more viable. You can almost always view the author of the content you are viewing in the history page and see who was working on it last.

You can also check the date and see if the content is just plain old. If the content is out of date and useless, you may want to delete it or set it to be updated. Adding a tag to tell other users it needs new information or adding it to the changes list can help tell your members that the page needs to be worked on next.

If the content of a page is not out of date, what about the relevance of that content? A major problem on many wikis is redundancy. If the content appears on another page, make sure to combine what is dissimilar and delete the rest. If the page is a stub of an administrative reminder, file it away somewhere out of the way.

Another major problem you may encounter is dead links. If a page is created and has no links on it, is there a way to make links and tie it back into your Web site or is it literally a dead end of information? Additionally, do any other pages connect to it? On a wiki, pages need to connect to each other. If there exists a lone stub page that has no role, it needs to be integrated or removed.

Finally, make sure the content of the page is meaningful. If a page only has 100 words of content on it, it probably does not warrant the existence of an entire page. You can either integrate the content back into another page or you can delete it completely. Before deletion though, always contact the author and ask them if they have more content to add before the page is removed. If

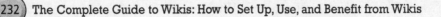

you can come up with enough to keep the page alive, it is worth saving most of the time.

Your Members

Your members are going to be the frontline against most of these issues as you will not be able to go through every single page of content in a wiki and maintain it personally. However, you need to be sure they are all trained properly and know what to look for as they write, edit, and change the wiki to conform to the editorial guidelines that have been set.

The best way to go about this is not simply to support those users who join your wiki and work on it, but to train a few select wiki users to be the frontline in maintaining the content and to report directly to you as needed. To do this, you may set up a few posts such as editors, managers, and contributors who directly work with the content. Here are a few steps to setting up and maintaining this kind of control over your wiki and your users:

- **Guidelines** — There need to be clear and well posted guidelines throughout the wiki to help users know exactly what it is they are supposed to be doing. If you need a certain structure for pages, post it in multiple locations. Always tell your users what you want to see and maintain a close eye on it. The same goes for those who edit your content. Make sure they understand what to look for, how to prune, and what needs to be deleted versus what needs to be saved.

- **Special Access** — If certain people need to have certain access to certain parts of your wiki, make sure they have access. This includes those users who need to be able to edit or update locked pages, those who should be able to lock down pages, and if you have editorial control over categories or whole sections, those areas as well.

- **Discussion** — Lieutenants and top editors should be constantly in conversation with the wiki owner, maintaining a dialogue about major changes, problems that might pop up, and anything else that might affect how the wiki is run and what needs to be done at any given time.

- **Top Users** — Top contributors and effective editors should be rewarded for their time with badges, accolades, or enhanced roles. Not only does this give them something for the time they are donating to your wiki, it maintains their presence on your wiki, ensuring they keep up the good job.

Wiki owners who maintain a solid team of contributors and editors are not only able to keep up with the change log and the constant maintenance that goes into a wiki, but also are much more capable of keeping an eye on more of their users.

Training Documents

One of the key factors that have been brought up in this book multiple times is having the right documentation for training in place throughout the wiki. But, it is important to know what that training documentation looks like and how to present it to users without making the wiki seem too much like a locked down, rule-guided project.

Wikipedia has always done a good job of maintaining style guides, editorial guidelines, and a series of tutorials on wiki markup and layouts. It would behoove any wiki owner to do the same for their wiki. Even if you just link directly to the Wikipedia guidelines, you can maintain a more regular sense of order and control over how the wiki looks without exerting as much effort if more and more of your users understand how the wiki is supposed to look, and are prepared and outfitted to enforce it for you.

Getting a Good Crew On Board

While earlier content in this book has already touched upon the process of finding and recruiting individuals to help with the creation and management of content, there is still one more highly valuable role that you are going to need to fill as you develop your wiki. This is the role of technical advisor, administrator, or guru — however they like to be called. If you work in an office setting and have access to IT support, this is not going to be an issue because your organization will probably require that you use in-house resources. However, if you are starting your own wiki for content or community purposes, you may need to go out and find someone who knows their way around a server and can help you develop your wiki effectively.

The first thing to remember is that a wiki is installed and runs on a Web server. It is completely unlike anything you are used to using on your home desktop or laptop and thus requires a very careful and well-trained approach. To effectively find someone who knows enough about wikis to maintain your server and your installation, there are a few things you should look for.

- **Administration** — Your new helper should be able to not only control and administrate the system on which your wiki will be running but the server and Internet in general. You will need them to be able to quickly and easily adapt and make decisions about the technical side of things so that you can focus more intently on the content and development side of things.

- **Programming and Databases** — They should know all of the programming languages we have discussed already in this book including Perl, PHP, Java, and HTML. Additionally, being able to access and work with databases will be very helpful for you here.

- **Security Work** — They should know how to integrate and use Internet security protocols to help your wiki remain that much safer.

- **Backup** — They should know how to back up your wiki, maintain those backups, and keep your server generally healthy so that it does not crash and if it does crash, they can get it back for you in a minimal amount of time.

When you hire someone who knows what they are doing, it is going to show in the finished product. Hiring students or hobbyists will almost always come back to haunt you, so be ready for anything and get a pro.

Full Time or Part Time

For the most part, you probably do not need to hire someone full time to help you out with this part of your wiki. Almost 99 percent of the time, you will not have many technical problems. However, the initial setup and any future issues that may occur are going to require someone skilled in the arts of server-side operations to maintain and control your wiki when necessary. There are a few options there then:

- **Find a Freelancer** — One of the easiest and most common ways to do this is to hire a freelance programmer who meets all of your criteria from a site like **www.elance.com** or **www.guru.com** where they tend to congregate, looking for work. It should not cost you too much as a wiki installation might take all of two hours to complete. This can be harder if you have technical problems later, but in many cases you can set up a deal where the freelancers make themselves available when you need them for a certain fee.

- **Use an In-House Tech** — If you are a teacher or an office manager, finding an in-house solution is going to be a bit easier than going out and hiring someone (largely because of the rules you are forced to live by). While in-house IT support can be hard to get when you need it, try to find

- **Find a Friend** — If all else fails, find a friend who knows a thing or two about programming and servers. Not everyone has a friend who knows enough or is willing to help out, but in today's computer-heavy age, the odds are getting better and better that someone in your family or immediate circle of friends knows a thing or two about the technical side of things.

In the end, make sure to find someone well versed who can make themselves available if you ever have trouble with your wiki and who really knows what they are doing. It is well worth your while in the long run to start off with a clean, efficient installation rather than trying to stumble through it on your own.

The Administrative Tasks

There are a slew of administrative tasks that you will be called upon to complete every day, week, month, and year and it can be a bit overwhelming to keep track of them all. Any Web site owner will usually have a good log or schedule that allows them to keep track of these tasks so they can mark them off at each interval as they are completed. Here is a listing of tasks broken down by increment and when they need to be completed to help establish the maintenance routine that will keep every good wiki up and running for years to come:

Daily

Each day, you are going to need to run through a number of different tasks to keep the wiki operational and effective. The first of these tasks is management of users. To have a good amount of users in a wiki who are able to contribute and help edit the content, regular run-throughs of new user submissions must be reviewed and approved to allow new users into the wiki. While most wikis allow automatic access, you will need to maintain a close eye on user names, anything that needs to be fixed, locking spam accounts, and much more.

Rolling back problems and changes that need to be removed is another daily task that should be kept in mind at all times. On any given day you could be vandalized and so rollbacks should be done as needed. Finally, you should be sure to back up your wiki daily if it is large enough to have daily changes. As soon as you could lose something by not backing up every day, you should start backing up every day.

Weekly

Weekly maintenance will include a number of very important tasks that do not necessarily need to be done daily but are nearly as important. The top tasks in this category include:

- **Group Management** — Keep track of groups and who is in them. Add and remove users as necessary, set your permissions, and change anything that is not currently working.

- **Prune Obsolete Content** — Go through pages once a week and look for anything that is obsolete. You may not have time to go through every page in your wiki, but if you do this weekly, you will be able to maintain a steady flow throughout the pages to see what is current and what is not.

- **Check Links** — Again, checking all the links in a wiki is incredibly time consuming, but going back through a few of them and making sure vital ones such as those on the front page are all active is important to do at least once a week.

Monthly

The monthly tasks are a bit more involved and do not necessarily need to be done on the same day each month (lest too much time is devoted to them), but they should each be completed at least once every month when possible:

- **Structural Assessment** — Make sure the structure of the wiki is still effective for the current build. If your business is growing or your content wiki is changing, you may need to rethink how the structure has been put together and how it interacts with the various parts of the site.

- **Ontology Checks** — Check to make sure the ontology is still effective and changes to content or the way that content is organized have not created cause to alter or reorganize the ontology, categorization, or linking within your wiki.

- **Check for New Content and Webs** — Look for new content in your wiki that could benefit from the building of a new Web. This allows for a bit more diversity of content each month as it will be reassessed every 30 days as needed.

- **Prune Old Pages** — Any pages that can be absorbed by other pages, deleted outright, or trimmed should be pulled out and assessed once a month at least. If the pages were not caught or dealt with during weekly maintenance this is a good time to do it.

- **Look for Heavy Use Pages** — Any pages that see a lot of traffic, a lot of edits, and a lot of argument should be seen to at least once a month. This will ensure that messy content, confusing changes, or subtle vandalism can be taken care of as it occurs and that nothing is left half finished.

- **Cut Out Redundancies** — If content is showing up in multiple locations, start compiling it and cutting out redundant pages. If the same content is appearing across multiple pages and sections, it may need to be restructured to fit into a new Web.

Annual

The annual tasks you complete are going to be the big picture ones that will allow you to step back and make sure everything being done with the wiki is still effective, still useful for your ultimate goals, and that the overall purpose of the wiki has not changed. It is a good time to celebrate your wiki's birthday, to look into other wiki systems and engines that may be available, and to rethink how your wiki is structured and how the information is being used. While these things may come up regularly throughout the year, having a once annual time in which to reassess the way your wiki is operating is going to be one of the better ways to be sure that you are not making any major mistakes, going down the wrong path, or simply getting complacent with the operation of your Web site.

Conclusion

Wiki maintenance and management is incredibly important. It can be very easy to get complacent about a wiki and how it operates very quickly. With so many people doing much of the work on their own, a wiki owner may think they do not need to do anything and that is when the problems will start to occur. To be ready for anything, you need to ensure you do not create problems through inaction. Perform regular maintenance, hire someone who is proficient and professional, and make sure installation goes off as smoothly as possible.

[[CHAPTER 12]]

Wiki Obstacles

There are going to be problems. I dare you to create and operate any Web site without running into problems. However, you are going to be able to avoid many of these problems by educating yourself as to what you need to expect and how to manage the problems that do arise. Things like mass use and the growth of a brand are both huge scalability issues that people tend to run into with popular wikis. Maintaining income and managing outward cash flow is tough as well and will become issues in the long run.

Wiki Adoption and the Hindrance Factors

Already discussed in the chapter about wiki promotion to some degree, wikis are an incredibly valuable tool with unprecedented growth potential but because of how they work and how many users you need to acquire before you are going to rightfully gather any kind of a following, there are some serious issues that come up when you start talking about adoption. People have to want to use your wiki and while functionality and promotion are vital keys, you are also going to have some serious issues to overcome no matter how much work you put into the site before anyone is willing to give up their time and energy for your wiki.

Different People and What They Bring

Every wiki has a slew of different people coming into it. That is the very nature of a wiki — a community tool that will be used by dozens if not hundreds or thousands of different people to do a variety of different tasks, and generally speaking they are all there for different reasons. Being able to manage all those different people with all their different goals and purposes is one of the major issues that all wiki owners need to be able to handle to maintain an effective hold of their site.

To start with, it is important to know what everyone might want out of the wiki. Here are a few different archetypes for the users of a wiki and what they bring to the site and what they want from the site:

The Researcher

Many people come to wikis simply to use them, researching content they may need for any number of purposes. If you have a content wiki and find a good niche, expect a huge number of these types of people to pop up, partaking of information freely without contributing to the site. This is a good thing. They represent traffic, potential income (for those wikis with ads) and a great way to grow the name. They may also help out with basic edits to spelling, grammar, and structure that they notice while reading content.

The Discusser

Many people will drop into a wiki to discuss issues related to the content. There may be a host of message boards and chat rooms out there, but the discussion pages of wikis are full of people interested in, ignited by, and willing to discuss carefully the merits of a discussion topic. It makes for a great location to share one's opinions, introduce new ideas, and try to convince others of a point of view. These individuals will often be much more active on discussion pages than in actually editing any content so the main issue with them is maintaining a civil tone, keeping controversy to a minimum, and ensuring they do not start editing content to match their opinions.

The Professional

Professional editors and contributors are the individuals you strive to capture for your wiki. These are the doctors who edit surgery pages on Wikipedia, the TV writers who edit synopses on television wikis, and the programmers who update documentation on programming wikis. The biggest problem with professional contributors is that they will often clash with other contributors when opinions do not match up. It is vital to maintain a close eye on content that does not fit together and remind users of the value of the discussion page to hash these things out.

The Vandal

Vandals are the worst kind of user and are only out to change things on a wiki to make jokes, elicit hate and fear, or simply cause problems. If you make your wiki open to the public, you will have vandals and they will cause problems. However, with the systems in place outlined in the chapters discussing security and maintenance, this problem can be minimized.

The Social Butterfly

The social butterfly is someone who comes to a wiki to make friends, become part of a community, and be a useful part of your team. You will find a number of these individuals in any wiki staff and they tend to end up in the top tier of the most useful members of the wiki. These individuals rarely cause problems, enjoy helping the wiki owner, and quickly come to see the wiki as a personal responsibility. The only time you will have trouble with this type of user is if too many people take on a personal role in the wiki and their interests start to clash with each other.

There are of course other kinds of users out there that will ultimately fit into the system created by a wiki or clash with it. Regardless, being able to work with all types of users — and to remove those users who are problematic — is a major goal for every wiki owner faced with user-related issues.

Web Hindrance

Another major problem that may arise in getting your wiki out there is finding the right avenue to develop it. While developing a good niche and creating a market for your wiki is a vital first step for any wiki, wiki owners also need to recognize the value of creating information that will naturally fit into and work with the Web site into which that information is being added. Here are a few common hindrances to wiki adoption and what they represent for a wiki owner just getting started:

Search Engine Placement

Getting a wiki placed within a search engine is a very important aspect of gathering traffic, building interest, and creating a surge of new users who will help to develop a wiki to become a more profitable time investment. However, when search engines do not cooperate this can become very hard. Some topics as well as some formats will just not do well in search engines right away. High spam frequency words such as gambling, pharmaceuticals, adult-related topics, or entertainment will all set off alerts with search engines and slow down listings. High competition will also hurt chances of listing well right away in a search engine. To overcome this, wiki owners must step back and think big, allowing the fact that it might take time to list well and continuing with SEO tactics listed earlier in this book.

Existing Competition

On the Internet, competition is a major factor at all times, no matter what topic you decide to build your wiki around. It is nearly impossible to find and capitalize on a new niche and even then, someone else may jump into the niche within a few days following your lead. So, new content, new members, and constant promotion are necessary compete in a tough, overcrowded online community of content.

Public Interest

Drumming up any public interest in a topic can be hard. It takes time to develop a basic interest in the content from the start, making sure that there is an actual audience out there. From there, wiki owners must put into place multiple strategies to build their audience, create new interest, and maintain that interest or the wiki can quickly fail.

Branding

Having a brand name or a useful image that will appeal to the target audience always helps when a new Web site goes up, especially before it is big enough to have the kind of content it needs to draw users on its own merits. Without proper branding and promotion it can be hard to capture any attention.

Professional Interest

Finding other wiki owners, bloggers, columnists, and Internet professionals to point out a new wiki, use that wiki, or promote it on its merits alone can be hard. The endorsement of an online professional is incredibly valuable but not always easy to obtain. While not a direct hindrance, it is a major boon if a wiki owner can find someone to vouch for their new site.

An Audience

One of the biggest issues that people tend to have with wiki adoption is finding an audience that wants to use their wiki. This means you need to go out and track down people who are going to actively use the wiki and that are not going to be fair-weather users. You do not want people who are waiting for the next big thing that will not do much work until they can just go in and make edits to pages that others have done the hard work on.

There are of course multiple other hindrances that might pop up for a new wiki that is trying to get off the ground. The majority of the issues in this chapter are related to content and community wikis. Process wikis have the basic issues of participation by an unwilling audience to deal with as well and all wikis have content issues, requiring a solid set of seed content to draw users in.

Whatever issues being faced, effective, intelligent planning will always go a long way in making sure that a wiki is able to overcome adoption and hindrance factors and create an audience.

CASE STUDY: JEREMY WILLIS

Jeremy Willis is a wiki programmer who has worked extensively for corporate clients in converting their projects into wiki-based operations, allowing them much easier, more streamlined methods of starting, operating, and maintaining their databases of information. His take on the current growth of the industry takes a longer, more contemplative perspective:

"I have been working with wikis for the past five years, and I have to say that I expected a bit more out of them by now," Willis said. "I think the biggest problem is that people do not quite understand or embrace the idea of shared information. Teachers still ban kids from using wikis as research tools, companies still think they are too easy to vandalize, and Web site owners still want to control their content in ways that they really cannot any more. At first I thought we'd see a major change over in a couple of years. Now, I do not think we will see the full embracing of wiki technology until everyone can get past the whole idea of them being problematic due to their open nature."

Mass Use and How to Grow a Brand Without Oversaturation

Whenever something new is created, there is an automatic risk that it might grow too quickly, or that it might create a problem in which it reaches too many corners of the Internet and creates too wide of a presence for itself without scaling properly to handle that newly found interest. It might sound like an amazing thing to suddenly have 2,000 users on a brand new wiki, but if the server cannot handle those users, the wiki's owner cannot manage that much content, or the users do not have the necessary training to add that content, things can fall apart very quickly.

Mass use of a wiki is the goal for many new wikis, especially content and community wikis, but it is vital that the systems needed to manage and control that flow of new content and the volume of new users is put into place before such a thing occurs. There are a few easy ways to ensure this happens:

Minimize Early Advertising — Do not start a new wiki when there is only one person managing it by throwing up $5,000 in advertising and getting unheard of new bouts of traffic into the site. Start small with basic search engine optimization, a little advertising, and the natural traffic increase that these will bring.

Create a Scaling Plan — Always have a plan in place for how the wiki will scale as it grows larger. Know the costs of upgrading servers and upgrade accounts at least 40 percent sooner than necessary. For example, if your monthly bandwidth is 10 GB of content, and you use up 6 GB of that bandwidth, upgrade your service before you get any closer to the cap. If you wait until you are at 9 GB to upgrade, your server might go down before you have a chance to upgrade the next time around. The same is true for the server itself and the technology supporting it. A shared server is rarely sufficient enough to handle 10,000 hits a day on your site. Make sure to have enough infrastructural support for whatever volume of users you expect to visit.

Have Technical Support — Always have at least one person on hand, either a friend, family member, or a paid freelancer or staff member, who can help with technical problems. If a server crashes or the Web site breaks or any number of other technical problems occur, there needs to be at least one person nearby who can get the wiki up and running again quickly and ensure minimal downtime.

Create a Team of Top Users — By scaling slowly, you can be sure that you have at least a small team of dedicated users who know exactly what they are doing and can help to maintain content before you have a stream of new users coming in and scrambling your pages. Imagine what would happen if you had 2,000 new users in the first month. Those users would tear pages apart with few, if any, people out there to help control it. If there were only 200 new users in the first month, you could talk to a half dozen of them and create a team of users who could monitor such growth more effectively.

Start Small and Grow

While the ultimate goal is always to grow and be successful, scaling and perspective are vital to any successful wiki. The most common and most effective way to build a wiki is to start small and have a good plan for growth. If you plan on becoming very large very quickly, ensure you have the resources in place, including paid staffers and programmers, to support and maintain the wiki as it grows.

How to Maintain Income or Manage Outward Cash Flow

While many wikis are built with the primary goal of maintaining a volume of content about a specific chunk of information or community group, there are instances in which wiki owners need to start considering things like income and costs. After all, a major Web site with a large sum of users can make money — that is the crux of Internet traffic these days. You make money simply by gathering people into a large space, usually by selling ad space on the page.

Many wiki owners choose to opt out of advertising, instead offering a free site that can be used by anyone with a donation button on the page to bring in just enough income to maintain the site. This is how Wikipedia has operated for the better part of a decade. It is ultimately up to the owner of a site if they will opt for advertising, donations, or no source of income at all to support their wiki.

However, there will be costs for almost any wiki that grows beyond a simple free hosted site and these costs can quickly change someone's mind about offering a free service when the first bills come in. Here are a few examples of the various costs that will start to accrue for a new wiki:

Server Maintenance (Or Hosting Fees) — The cost of hosting your wiki on a server or of upgrading a hosted wiki to a paid account for privacy will become an issue as soon as there are enough users to make it one. While hosted wiki fees are small (usually around $5), server fees can be much higher — anywhere between $10 and $300 each month.

Freelancing Costs — The cost to hire an Internet professional to help install or maintain a wiki is quite expensive. Most quality programmers are going to cost between $50 and $100 an hour and if something goes wrong, they might charge even more for specific tasks and repairs.

Your Time — The value of your own time can never be underestimated. It takes a lot of time and energy to maintain a wiki and not making any money while doing so can be hard to swallow.

Advertising — If you want the most possible people to see your new wiki, advertising is the best way to do so and it will cost money to have ads placed throughout search results, blogs, or other wikis.

In the end, there are a number of costs that add up quickly for a wiki operator. Having to pay those out of pocket can be hard to handle. Keep in mind that income is available online for anyone that can generate traffic. Something that is as simple as placing Google AdWords at the bottom of a page can generate small bits of income every time someone clicks on an ad.

Conclusion

All Web sites have obstacles. In fact, most have tremendous obstacles that are going to stand in the way of effective completion of certain tasks. Wikis are no different, but because so many people have come before you, it is easy to draw upon their knowledge and ensure your wiki is adopted quickly, develops at a decent pace, and never costs you more than it generates in income.

[[CHAPTER 13]]

Things You Can Do With Your Wiki and Where Wikis Are Headed

Wikis are an obvious future tool in the way in which they are currently being used. Throughout their history, they have been developed and manipulated for use in ways that few if any people would have anticipated and more new ways are constantly being developed. Those who are at the cutting edge of the trend will be able to more effectively maintain their hold on technology by thinking outside the box and working toward new and exciting applications.

Below you will find the top ten things currently being done with wikis alongside what is coming soon and the future of wikis and the wiki technology.

The Things You Can Do With Your Wiki

So, what is it about a wiki that is so special? What is it that so many users have found so drawing about the technology that it has grown so vastly in the last few years? In most ways, it is the versatility of the wikis out there, the technology that allows anyone to do pretty much anything they want with them. Open source, open platform software has more possibilities than even its creators can keep track of in most cases and wikis are no exception.

CASE STUDY: STEWART ELLIS

A regular wiki user and a huge fan of how much easier Wikipedia and other sites made college research papers, Stewart Ellis has started using wikis to do much more than just research; he finds new, exciting ways to integrate technology into his life:

"I first heard about Wikipedia when I was in college, probably five or six years ago," Ellis said. "It was supposedly an encyclopedia that anyone could access or edit and I was intrigued, mainly because every other source of information before that was closed and required you to pay (Anyone remember trying to use Britannica or that mess Microsoft® had up back in the day?) Wikipedia was free so it was interesting and I started using it to research my papers."

"So, that was probably when I first started using wikis, when they were useful for me to do my schoolwork much faster," he continued. "I later started using them for my work, doing basic research and keeping track of things simply enough. I also started one up when I got married, though it did not get used as much as I would have liked — it was still a great way of keeping everyone informed about changes to the wedding as we were making them (and there were plenty of them)."

Event Planning

One of the most fundamental uses for a wiki that has really caught on in recent years is the use of them to plan events of many shapes and sizes. The simplest and most commonly cited of these is a wedding. More and more people are turning away from one-stop wedding planners and allowing their friends and families to help them plan through online technology that allows them to organize ideas, resources, and plans in a single resource.

Wiki access can fast forward the planning of any number of events with ease. Putting together invitation lists or having people confirm an invitation can be as easy as posting a listing on a wiki so everyone can see it. Of course, this does not work if you want Uncle Jimmy and Cousin Tim to both come and one of them will not come if the other is there, but, in many cases, it can save a ton of money on invitations and a lot of time in organizing and sorting through all of the replies.

Regardless of how you use them, wikis are one of the most powerful organizational tools out there. They will make it much easier to get everyone together in a single place with ease. Just make sure you make it easy to edit and give instructions for those in your family that may not know how to use a wiki.

Interactive Photo Album or Multimedia Hub

Sharing photos with family members, loved ones, or coworkers can be hard, but a wiki makes it much easier to contribute your share of the memories and allowing anyone access to them. When you upload them to the wiki they are much easier to access and thus you can quickly and easily logon and edit the albums, adding information about each person in a photo, changing the order, or simply adding your own images. Video databases can work in similar ways if your wiki supports multimedia uploads.

Tribute or Memorial

Being able to log on to a Web site and place a tribute or memorial to a loved one is a growing trend that allows everyone that knew someone important to them to add their thoughts. Oftentimes, memorial services are reserved for those who have the time and the closeness to step forward for a loved one and many times the only people who can share their sentiments are those closest to the deceased. An online tribute on the form of a wiki allows anyone to quickly and easily post their thoughts and share them with the world.

Write a Book

In what is becoming a quickly growing and fast moving trend throughout the technical world, online collaboration is happening more and more through private wikis. A single installation with limited access set up on a private server can have tremendous uses in collaborative projects such as the writing of a book. Two individuals, who both track their changes, can easily write parts of a book, add to chapters written by their partner, and make edits or notes on other parts without there being any concerns over lost drafts, missing sections, or a lack of participation by either side. It allows for long-distance collaboration in new and exciting ways as well. This is becoming much more popular for technical projects as well where a book might have multiple authors.

Present Documentation for an Organization

Documentation of a process, resource, or past events in an organization is always a time consuming and paper wasting activity, but wikis are making it much easier. Some companies have already started implementing methods in which one individual may maintain a wiki for recent documentation while their co-workers are required to post weekly their updated progress and documentation. Other companies are using wikis as collaborative work spaces to post documentation for new trainees. This allows for faster updating, more up-to-date training, and company-wide access to what would have been closed resources. It cuts back on miscommunication and develops a much closer, more effective relationship between branches or departments without wasting anyone's time or money in the process.

Teach More Effectively

This does not necessarily need to apply only to teachers and as such is quickly becoming a much more universal tool in many ways. While most individuals with college degrees today either did not or barely used a computer in the classroom, today's high school students revolve much of their learning around the computer, oftentimes even getting one from the school to use at home. Having students download, complete, and access their homework via a wiki saves resources, makes it easier to get homework to sick students, speeds up response, and allows students to complete coursework in a cyberspace they grew up with, one they are more comfortable with than the classroom in many cases. Wikis are also being used to great effect to showcase the work and roles that a student can have in the classroom, putting some students in responsible positions, while others learn the value of collaborative work — the cornerstone of the effective worker in modern society.

Project Management

If you have ever tried to manage a project without the use of software of some sort, you know how hard it can be to effectively combine resources from multiple departments and put them into a single streamlined interface. It is a good reason why project managers are often so overworked and stressed out (and underpaid). Wikis are incredible tools that can allow for much more effective project management and a level of open-endedness with clients that has never before been seen. You can organize everything in one place so all departments and individuals can see it.

You can streamline the workflow and cut down on e-mail and document management. You can tell everyone where the project is at so schedules are always synchronized without having to remind anyone. You can involve everyone easily because they will all have access to the wiki in real time. It cuts out a lot of the problems big projects will sometimes have and replaces them with streamlined resources to make everything that much easier.

Collaborating with Clients

While many businesses and those who are not used to the technology will chafe at the idea of a client working directly with them on a project, a wiki is a great way to allow such collaboration without it ever slowing down the project. On a wiki, you can show your clients exactly where you are in a project, which allows them to make changes and suggestions that match your progress without interrupting the flow of the project. If they do not know your progress, they might make suggestions that do not fit your timeline and only slow everyone down, but by incorporating them into the wiki, they can suggest, give feedback, and be involved. It increases customer satisfaction, streamlines editing and changes, and ensures less miscommunication in the long run.

Means of Getting Public Feedback

Something that some have suggested and many have supported for government use and for additional use in wide companies is the use of a wiki to solicit public feedback. Producing information and allowing users to access and comment on it in real time, providing their own takes, developing ideas with their neighbors and bouncing them back and forth off of politicians, lawmakers, or simply corporation operators. It can work on a smaller scale as well and is often used to produce faster results, more complete feedback, and a wide array of accessible, easily discussed comments on a topic with ease.

Group Motivation for an Event

One thing that many people struggle with when it arises is finding the motivation to complete or join in on an event — things like marathons, New Year's resolutions or National Novel Writing Month. Regardless of your reason for performing in such an event or annual ritual, it almost always helps to have other people who can motivate you and a wiki is a great way to connect, sharing your stories, developing training plans, finding people to join you in running, exercising off that Christmas ham, or writing Chapter 12. No matter how you look at it, the resources a wiki provides are ideal for such needs.

Other Uses for a Wiki

While the list above is a nice collection of the most common and yet least considered uses for a wiki, there are a slew of other ways you can put a wiki to use for you and in your life just like many others. Here are a few more examples:

- Play chess with numerous people
- Create product manuals (see Motorola's Q)
- A current history of civilization
- Write a business plan
- Write a script or screenplay
- Record and maintain notes of conference calls and meetings
- Notes and ideas for YouTube videos or podcasts

- Magazine article writing
- Sharing your love of a certain item or TV show

The list can go on and on with literally hundreds or even thousands of different ways in which you can honestly enjoy the world around you better through a wiki. It is the face of the new generation of technology and it is already changed much of how we do things.

The Future of Wikis

So, that brings us to the future of the wiki, an often discussed and rarely agreed upon question that many technology gurus have weighed in on and very few of them have managed to agree upon in any specific form. Five years ago, few people would have figured that even Wikipedia would have been this successful or that wikis would finally be common place and used by everyone instead of just a few select individuals who used them for programming collaboration.

So, what will we be using them for in five years that we cannot imagine today? The odds are that there will not be many more innovative uses for wikis in the weeks, months, or years to come. However, what you can count on is that wikis will find a widespread usage and understanding among users that other technologies already enjoy. There are a few reasons for this.

First of all, a wiki is much easier to understand and to use than a Web page based in HTML. Anyone can pick up and start working with a wiki in a few minutes while a code-based Web site would take a few days to figure out the basics of. That makes it accessible to nearly anyone, including children, and it will thus be used on a wider scale. As the current generation of students and graduates begins to mature into corporate and educational America, you can expect a new bent on technology use in the classroom as well, as the current trendiness starts to subside in favor of the standardized uses of that technology. Think back to the mid-90s when the Internet was still a "really cool" thing to have in school or at work. Today, it is absolutely required and no one thinks about it in any other way. Wikis will soon take up a similar mantle, being just another tool on everyone's desktop like e-mail or Google.

Wide use of wikis and wider understanding of the technology will undoubtedly curtail into a much wider appreciation of the technology and, with time, you can expect there to be a burgeoning of new software models and integration options for wikis. Much as Google Desktop and similar tools brought Web browsing and access to every part of your computer, expect wiki access and editing to become a desktop activity (as in the rumored new features found in Windows 7 and the long-rumored next upgrade the Mac OS).

Whether standardization is going to happen for wikis is hard to know. Until a major company steps up and chooses a format to use that steamrolls the rest or creates their own, the wide array of options will continue. Open source is definitely still going to be the way of the future though, so do not worry about having to pay for your next wiki platform in a few years. They will always be free to use and access.

In the end, a wiki is many things, but mostly it is a representation of the world in which we live — the current climate of mass collaboration and worldwide composition of ideas. There are no boundaries anymore and when put to proper use, anyone anywhere can do essentially anything with a wiki. On the road we are currently traveling, those borders will only continue to shrink with time and the possibilities will become more endless. From video and audio integration to free-form image editing, to worldwide collaboration on creative projects, wikis are just starting their rapid ascension into the consciousness and valuation of modern society. In the next few years you are going to see the world take to this technology like it took to search engines, e-mail, and social networking, and the results of that transition are going to fundamentally change how all of us see and use the Internet. You can all but guarantee it.

Conclusion

Wikis are an extraordinary online resource and if the last decade is any indication, they will likely continue to grow in number and importance throughout the next decade. The idea of collaboration, which was once laughed at as being too riddled with potential pitfalls, has become the concept of the day, with classrooms, small businesses, major corporations, and regular Joes everywhere using it to break down barriers and try new things.

With this book in hand, you should be prepared to not only start your own wiki, but to implement strategies, initiate creativity, and develop new ideas about how to use them in the future. Businesses are very quickly learning that wiki platforms are not only cheaper and easier; they are more effective in keeping track of projects and keeping employees interconnected. Teachers are learning that wikis can bring every student into the fold instead of those eager to participate while also providing new ways to learn and entertaining ways to educate. Community leaders, club organizers, brides and grooms, and thousands more are learning that they can share information with one another faster than ever before and streamline dozens of actions that once gave headaches. Wikis have solved many, many problems and look to continue doing so in the foreseeable future as they continue to become more viable for more complex processes.

Using a wiki is not just a chore or an educational exercise. It is a chance to enjoy something new, meet new people, and share ideas across borders that are falling at a faster rate each and every year.

CASE STUDY: CECILE GOLDSMITH

Cecile Goldsmith is a programmer who has worked on numerous wiki projects including open source additions to MediaWiki and Socialtext along with enterprise solutions for multiple Fortune 500 companies. Currently living in Seattle, Wash., Goldsmith has a bright outlook on the future of wikis and what they will bring to the Internet as it develops further into the Web 2.0 era:

"Wikis are going places that we have not even begun to think about yet," Goldsmith said. "The wiki platform is so agile — so effective at adapting to the different ways in which it can be used that I doubt we would be able to think of everything they could be used for if we tried."

"One thing I have been seeing a lot of lately is the application of wiki concepts and technology to ideas that wouldn't have originally matched what wikis were made for," Goldsmith added. "Things like medical consulting done by doctors who share ideas or repairing cars by sharing information on what sounds tend to mean what problems. Even when not using a wiki platform, we are seeing people learning to work together more often and more effectively. Honestly, I have been blown away with just how much people have been getting out of the technology and what it means for the future of the Internet."

[[APPENDIX A]]

Resources and Web sites

Here, you will find a slew of detailed bits of information with tools, lists of wikis, and links to each of them, allowing you to visit and read more about the huge volume of options that are available online for those wanting to start a new wiki:

List of Wikis:

The following is a list of wikis that can be used either as a hosted service or to install on your own server and create a new wiki:

Hosted Wiki Web sites:

PBworks — Easy to use, quick personal wiki Web site that allows for 30 second online startup with special options for educational, business, and personal sites.

OttoWiki — This site allows you to build a personal wiki that tracks projects and collaborative documents online.

Wikispaces — Easy-to-create wiki hosting service for personal, educational, and business wikis.

Wetpaint — One of the largest of the current spate of wikis, this site lets you build both private and public Web sites.

ServerSideWiki — This wiki service is a bit more advanced and works toward creating incredibly fast and easy-to-use wikis.

Netcipia — A private wiki and blog creation site that allows you to invite others to join in and participate with you.

Zwiki — Another simple free wiki site with large communities of users and free tools to collaborate with them.

Near-Time — Collaborative wiki projects for use with businesses, customers, and friends easily over a wide array of topics.

LittleWiki — Public or private wiki options for anyone to access and edit.

ProjectForum — A service that provides easy-to-use wiki services while also allowing you to download and install your own software alongside it easily.

Socialtext — A very popular, very simple wiki setup with mostly text and minimal interactivity. Has multiple plan options for businesses and groups.

Wikia — One of the largest online wiki communities with multiple different topic areas and some of the largest created wikis around — uses MediaWiki as its base platform.

Open Source Wiki Engines

ProjectForum — As listed above, a simple wiki platform for sharing ideas — also available to use on their hosted site.

XWiki — Quick and easy-to-install open source platform under the LGPL licensing method.

TWiki — A very highly regarded, more advanced wiki option that allows high-end business use and knowledge sharing with multiple plug-ins for advances uses.

OpenWiki — Open source wiki software designed around creating and operating workspaces for different users.

MediaWiki — Best known wiki software, used to back up sites like Wikipedia. Very easy to use and install and highly regarded for speed and efficiency.

List of Hosting Services

Along with the different types of wikis out there, you will find a slew of different hosting options for where to put your wiki and how to keep it operating. Here are a few of the more popular options on the market right now:

Site Ground — Site Ground starts at $5.95 a month, offers 750 GB of space and 7,500 GB of bandwidth along with free installation of major wiki engines like TWiki and MediaWiki, and has great customer service.

ServerFly — ServerFly provides $5.95 service with 200 GB of space and 2,000 GB of bandwidth and free installation of TWiki along with multiple tech services to help in setting up your site.

Host Monster — Host Monster offers service for $6.95 with 1,500 GB of space and 15,000 GB of bandwidth along with free installation of TikiWiki to your site and tech support to go with it.

Host Gator — Well known for their service throughout multiple different niches, Host Gator provides $6.95 service for 350 GB of space and 3,000 GB of bandwidth and installation of either Tiki-Wiki or PhpWiki to your server.

[[APPENDIX B]]

FAQs About Wikis

Because wikis are such a complex, evolving platform that has so many different ways to evolve and change as the years go by and your needs for them change, here are a few different frequently asked questions that often come up in regard to wikis and how they are used throughout the Internet:

Can someone edit anything I have written?

As daunting and terrifying as it may seem (especially after years of living in a world where the work you do is unique to you and absolute in almost every way), wikis can and will be edited by anyone regardless of who writes the original content. One of the biggest parts of getting used to working on a wiki is knowing that anything you write can and will be changed. However, something that all wiki users should remember is that users of a wiki are well known for recognizing and respecting quality work and ensuring nothing is mistreated or ignored when not merited.

You will quickly learn that in the modern age of collaboration and sharing, knowledge and productivity is not something that can be written out by one person and then held in stone for X amount of time. A wiki relies on the fluidity of information and the willingness and ability of everyone to volunteer and provide their knowledge without fear of it being destroyed by someone else.

How do I see changes to a wiki made by someone else?

Almost any wiki will have a means by which you can login and check on the changes they have made to a certain section. If you go to the History page on a wiki and look for the changes that have been made in recent days you will find that the wiki has been altered in many ways to include the different bits and pieces of information that a particular user changed. You can also look at the times and dates of their changes, what the pages looked like before their changes, or a total list of all changes that particular user may have made to the wiki.

How do I know when changes are made?

One of the most useful tools on a wiki, especially if you are monitoring a particular page (or multiple pages), is the notification feature that they almost all have. This feature will e-mail a set list of individuals who have asked to be notified whenever something is changed. Businesses and individuals use this feature on Wikipedia every day to monitor what people are saying about them (and edit it if necessary) and wiki owners can use this to monitor high density pages that might pose a particularly large problem.

Should I change something I do not like?

The big question is not whether you like or dislike something someone else has written. The question that needs to be asked before any changes are made to a wiki at any given point is whether what another individual has written has any merit. So, ask yourself why you do not like what was written. Is it because it is poorly written? In this case, you may want to rewrite or edit the content to look better. Is it because the content goes against what you believe in? You may want to go to the discussion page and talk with fellow editors then before you start making potentially controversial changes. Is it because the content is irrelevant or poorly placed? You may want to review where the content could go instead or how it could be altered to more effectively fit into a page.

The first thing that should be asked before any edits are made is whether content can be made better. If it can, try to improve before you tear down anything on a wiki. The goal of collaboration is to grow, not to repeatedly take apart and restructure content from the ground up. If you are able to do this and to relate this frame of mind to your users, the goal of your wiki will more often than not be met.

What if people just start changing everything each other has written?

This rarely if ever happens and for good reason. Wikis are an interesting creation that many people tend to worry about more than the actual problems dictate. Not only do most editing guidelines dictate that users should not do this; common decency tells someone that they should not just delete whatever they see that they do not like. It is not very nice and while it might seem like there are a lot of people out there intent on destroying what you have created, there really are not.

However, if this does happen, wikis have a whole slew of tools to make things more secure. Not only can changes be rolled back to previous versions with the click of a button, users can easily see who has been making changes, block them or delete them, and in many cases, lock out a particular wiki page so that only a select few can edit it if such things occur.

How do I know everything is accurate?

This is the big question that has been driving the argument against wikis like Wikipedia for years now. When it first launched, Wikipedia was a cool idea. When it became the monstrous source of information that it currently is, it suddenly went from cool idea to major controversy as trained historians and academics began to chafe at the idea that a select few individuals would be capable of or willing to maintain knowledge as impartially as academia has been doing for centuries.

On the flip side, people like Wikipedia creator Jimmy Wales have called the site the most accurate encyclopedia in the world. It is certainly the largest, but whether it is more accurate has never really been settled. However, in the end, the argument comes down to how much trust can be put in the masses. As it turns out, for the most part people are every bit as good at maintaining accuracy as individuals with degrees. With a few key safeguards in place and the whole of human knowledge being funneled into a single resource, wikis are generally very accurate when allowed to exist naturally with a bit of basic oversight.

Who should be the administrator of the wiki?

Every wiki needs someone to oversee it. It is a requisite based solely on the fact that nothing can be run without someone overseeing the maintenance, handling, and general wellness of a system without problems occurring. So, it is a good idea that someone well trained and willing to spend the necessary time and energy it takes to watch over the wiki is in charge. You can do it yourself if you have the technical expertise, but expect to need a couple hours a day to watch over it.

No one, however, will ever fully control the wiki. Once a wiki is started and let loose into the wild, it will become the property and provenance of the people using it. This makes administration much easier and at the same all that much harder. After all, no one likes to give up control over something they have put so much time and energy into.

What do I do to get people from e-mail over to a wiki?

One of the biggest problems that people have in organizations is getting users to switch over from e-mail to use of a wiki. The problem here lies largely in the fact that they even try to get people to switch. For the most part, there is little if any reason to force a switch over from one system to another. E-mail and wikis can work well in tandem if properly implemented.

What a wiki does is provide an open forum for collaboration and sharing that is much more easily viewed, worked with, and organized than e-mail. Files, processes, and projects are all right there for everyone to see and work with in a wiki. However, e-mail is used for more direct conversations, requests, and discussions. Memos and interpersonal conversations do not really work via a wiki — it is not made for conversations. So, by combining a wiki with e-mail, posting memos with e-mail addresses, and e-mailing new updates to a wiki along with notifications to members of a particular Web site, you can integrate the two. Instead of facing so much resistance from those that want to keep their e-mail, you can draw them into using a wiki by putting them together.

What if something on a wiki does not make any sense? How do I change it?

If you come across something on a wiki that just plain does not make any sense, your first goal should be to establish the exact problem. If it does not make sense because it is poorly written, try rewriting it with proper grammar, punctuation, and purpose. If it does not make sense because it really does not make any sense, see if you can discern who made the edit via the history page and discuss what they were trying to do with it. If that does not work, try leaving general discussion notes in thread mode so that people can help you work out what the problem is and create a solution. While changing something outright is always an option, it should never be your first choice. You do not want to step on toes or remove information that might be useful if written a little more clearly.

What makes a wiki different from project management software?

This is a very deep and complicated question for a few reasons. The most obvious differences are that wikis are much cheaper (or free), easier to learn and train, and Web-based. Project management software is often expensive, requires individual licenses for each user, and requires advanced, specific training that then results in the need for project managers who spend their entire days going through and updating the software.

The other major difference is collaboration. Most project management software has poorly implemented collaboration tools that are hard to use and require training or intranet access to work with. Wikis can be accessed anywhere and by anyone with minimal training and that makes collaboration much easier across the board. The two are coming closer together with many enterprise wikis being much more developed with project management tools so the line is blurring more and more, but wikis are still much more flexible.

Will an IT department be willing to add another system to their support list?

While it might seem daunting to even think about contacting IT and asking them about adding a new system to all that stuff they already maintain, many workplaces find that a wiki is actually welcomed by IT. First of all, it is easy to install and even easier to maintain. Second, it requires almost no work by IT after initial installation and regular backups. There are almost never any problems, the infrastructure can support huge numbers of users natively, and the basic integration of tools makes training and troubleshooting minimal. Compared to enterprise software that constantly has problems and needs help all the time, wikis are easy to deal with, plus most IT departments should already know how to install them, requiring very little additional time investment.

What about those who do not talk much or contribute — how do I get them to use the wiki?

The beauty of a wiki is that the innate nature of the software draws users in naturally in many ways. There will, however, be two types of users that will be hard to get behind the idea of using a wiki. The first is the individuals who are intimidated and made uneasy by technology in general. These individuals will need some basic instruction and motivation to make the change but with WYSIWYG editors and easy posting options, their complaints usually subside relatively quickly.

The second group is those that just do not like to actively voice their opinions or ideas because they are not as social as their peers or coworkers. These individuals can be given anonymity to speed up their use of the software, forced to use it through incentives, or allowed to observe for a while before they jump in. However you look at it though, most of the time most individuals will jump into the wiki format more easily than meetings or classes if only because it is slightly more anonymous. Such is the nature of the Internet — anonymity creates willingness to be involved.

[[BIBLIOGRAPHY]]

Albrycht. "Thinking About Wikis." 2006. Society for New Communications Review, **www.newcommreview.com**, January 28, 2009.

Anonymous. "Educational Wikis." **http://educationalwikis. wikispaces.com/Classroom+Wikis,** December 2, 2009

Anonymous. "List of Wiki Resources." **www.socialtext.net/lite/ page/medialiteracy/wiki_resources**, January 3, 2009

Anonymous. "My Brilliant Failure: Wikis in the Classroom." May, 2004. **http://kairosnews.org/node/3794**, January 30, 2009.

Anonymous. The Cool Cat Teacher Blog, December 2005. **http:// coolcatteacher.blogspot.com/2005/12/wiki-wiki-teaching-art- of-using-wiki.html**, January5, 2009.

Anonymous. "Using Blogs and Wikis in Business." **http://tech- net.microsoft.com/en-us/windowsserver/sharepoint/bb400751. aspx-2009**, January 24, 2009.

Anonymous. "What is Wiki?" June, 2002. **www.wiki.org**, January 24, 2009.

Anonymous. "Wiki History." **http://c2.com/cgi/ wiki?WikiHistory**, December 20, 2008.

Bartlett, Daniel J. MediaWiki. New York: O'Reilly Media Inc., 2008.

Broughton, John. Wikipedia: The Missing Manual. New York: Pogue Press, 2008.

Burrows, Terry. Blogs, Wikis, MySpace, and More: Everything You Want to Know About Using Web 2.0 but Are too Afraid to Ask. Chicago: Chicago Review Press, 2008.

Cashmore, Pete. "The Wiki Toolbox: 30+ Wiki Tools and Resources." **http://mashable.com/2007/07/16/wiki-toolbox/**, December 24, 2008

Confluence Enterprise Wiki, **www.atlassian.com/software/confluence/wiki.jsp**, January 13, 2009

Ebersbach, Anja; Glaser, Markus; et al. Wiki Web Collaboration. New York: Springer, 2008.

Educause Learning Initiative, "7 Things You Should Know About Wikis." July, 2005, **http://net.educause.edu/ir/library/pdf/ELI7004.pdf**, February 1, 2009.

Edward, Penny. "Managing Wikis in Business." September, 2007. **http://pennyedwards.files.wordpress.com/2007/10/final-report-september-2007.pdf**, January 15, 2009.

Gilbane Report. "Blogs and Wikis: Technologies for Enterprise Applications?" Vol 12, No10, 2005.

Goodnoe, Ezra. "How to Use Wikis for Business." August 8, 2005, Information Week. **www.informationweek.com/news/management/showArticle.jhtml?articleID=167600331**, January 5, 2009.

Lau, Kathlene. "Three Myths of Enterprise Wiki Deployment," January 28, 2009. **www.itworld.com/software/61612/three-myths-enterprise-wiki-deployment**, January 31, 2009.

Leuf, Bo and Cunningham, Ward. The Wiki Way – Quick Collaboration on the Web. New York: Addison-Wesley Professional, 2001.

Mader, Stewart. Wikipatterns. Denver: Wiley Publishing, 2007.

Marshall, Brian. "How Wikis Work." **http://computer.howstuff-works.com/wiki.htm,** December 10, 2008.

Rothbart, Jason. Future Changes/GroupSwim. January 27, 2009. **www.ikiw.org/2009/01/27/planning-a-collaborative-effort-why-its-crucial-to success/#more-4252,** January 29, 2009

Site Overview. **www.wikimatrix.org,** January 24, 2009.

Tapscott, Don; Williams, Anthony D. Wikinomics: How Mass Collaboration Changed Everything. New York: Portfolio Hardcover, 2006.

Wikipedia Overview. **www.Wikipedia.com,** January 15, 2009.

Wikispaces Overview. **www.Wikispaces.com,** January 15, 2009.

Woods, Dan and Thoeny, Peter. Wikis for Dummies. New York: For Dummies Publishing, 2007.

[[INDEX]]

S

Sandbox, 185, 35, 37, 46, 285

search box, 140, 158-159

search rankings, 156, 192, 195, 200

Searching, 24, 285

security, 78, 86, 89, 91-92, 103, 123, 144-145, 203, 206, 214, 218, 225, 235, 245, 7-8

SEO, 52-53, 71, 184, 188, 192, 196-197, 199-201, 204, 247, 285, 5

shared hosting, 218-219, 221

sidebar, 157-159

skins, 149, 160

social networks, 181, 197

Socialtext, 268, 279, 81-82, 90, 106, 266, 285

Software, 268-269, 276-278, 280-281, 54, 57, 61, 75, 78, 83-87, 89-92, 102-103, 105-106, 109, 111, 113, 116, 122-123, 125, 159-160, 21-22, 24, 28, 36, 206, 213-214, 220-226, 229, 255, 259, 263, 285, 6

space and time, 152

spam, 86, 181-182, 195, 199, 207, 226, 238, 247, 8

storage, 78, 81, 226

structure, 93, 99, 144, 149-154, 163, 170, 172, 174-175, 179, 32, 211, 229, 232, 239, 244, 7

stub lists, 169

subscriptions, 159

support pages, 155, 159

T

tags, 95, 138, 149, 158, 168, 170, 173-174, 35, 39, 230, 7

template, 161-163, 189-190, 46

themes, 62, 146, 149, 160

TiddlyWiki, 85, 90, 285